WELLINGTON'S HIDDEN HEROES

The Dutch and the Belgians at Waterloo

Veronica Baker-Smith

CASEMATE
uk

Oxford & Philadelphia

Published in Great Britain and
the United States of America in 2015 by
CASEMATE PUBLISHERS
10 Hythe Bridge Street, Oxford OX1 2EW, UK

and

908 Darby Road, Havertown, PA 19083, USA

Hardcover Edition: ISBN 978-1-61200-332-0
Digital Edition: ISBN 978-1-61200-333-7

A CIP record for this book is available from the British Library

Typeset and design by Casemate Publishers

Printed and bound in the UK by TJ International

For a complete list of Casemate titles, please contact:

CASEMATE PUBLISHERS (UK)
Telephone (01865) 241249
Fax (01865) 794449
Email: casemate-uk@casematepublishers.co.uk
www.casematepublishers.co.uk

CASEMATE PUBLISHERS (US)
Telephone (610) 853-9131
Fax (610) 853-9146
Email: casemate@casematepublishing.com
www.casematepublishing.com

For Susannah

Contents

Acknowledgements

The preparation of this book has incurred debts on both sides of the North Sea.

In the Netherlands I have had the privilege and pleasure of many hours of working in the Royal Archive at The Hague, where Drs. Charlotte Eymael, the Director, and her staff have been unfailingly courteous and immensely helpful in their suggestions. They have also allowed me to reproduce some important images from their collection which have not been seen in English work, and I thank them most sincerely. I am grateful also to the staff of the Nationaal Archief in The Hague and to the Historischcentrum in Zwolle. The interest shown in my work by Jan de Hond of the Rijksmuseum, Amsterdam, has been much appreciated, and his colleague, Eveline Sint Nicolaas was able to explain to me some of the finer points of the images from their collections. I also benefitted greatly from a long conversation with Jeroen van Zanten, whose recent biography of Koning Willem II has been an important resource. My friends, Maud Peereboom-Engelberts and Martien Kappers-den Hollander, have been assiduous in drawing contemporary material to my attention, and checking references for me. The tolerance shown by all of these to the presumptuous attempts of a *buitenlander* to expound their history will, I hope, be repaid by the recognition at last, on this side of the North Sea, of the true contribution made by their country to the climactic Campaign against Napoleon.

In England also the debts are considerable – first and foremost to Professor Saul David who has supported the project at all stages of its development, even to the extent of reading through the finished manuscript. His advice and encouragement have been both a stimulus and a reassurance. Anyone engaged in the study of such a major event as the Waterloo Campaign is, of course, indebted to the work of many others – the stimulus (and sometimes provocation) I received from them should be evident from my footnotes, but I also gratefully acknowledge them here Finally, and of course by no means least, I must thank Casemate, and especially my editor there, Clare Litt, for her commitment and her patient acceptance of a certain amount of technological inadequacy.

Introduction

THE DUKE OF WELLINGTON described the Battle of Waterloo as 'the most desperate business I ever was in ... I never was so near being beat'. The courage and sacrifice of British soldiers on 18 June 1815 has been rightly recognised and eulogised, but the fact that one-third of the Allied Army which gave him his narrow victory that day were actually subjects of the King of the Netherlands, Dutch, Belgian and German, is only now receiving any acknowledgement. As the two hundredth anniversary of the Waterloo Campaign is celebrated, this work reveals the vital contribution of those men through the analysis of Dutch sources – both primary and secondary – and some French ones, very few of which have been studied by English-speaking historians, except in translation. Such analysis uncovers a new side to the well-worn story.

The efforts of the Congress of Vienna to re-draw the map of Europe after twenty years of Napoleonic rule included the creation of 'the Netherlands', combining the ill-matched countries of Belgium and Holland (both previously annexed by France), and placing them under the rule of an untried prince of the House of Orange-Nassau. When the leisurely deliberations of the Congress were interrupted by Napoleon's return from exile on Elba, it was for Wellington, in the words of Tsar Alexander of Russia, 'to save the world again'; at the beginning of April 1815 he arrived in Brussels to take command of an army, consisting of roughly one-third British, one-third German (Hanoverian and King's German Legion) and one-third Netherlanders. The first two elements were familiar to him and he had commanded them before in the Peninsula – his five-year campaign against the French in Portugal and Spain – and elsewhere, but the third was an unknown quantity, and his distrust of it was to have a far-reaching, and almost disastrous, effect on the whole campaign.

The challenge for the Netherlands had begun eighteen months previously as the newly installed Prince-Sovereign attempted to build and equip an army while combining two disparate nationalities within it. His achievement is studied here, for the first time, in detail, and the difficulties of training and logistics examined, but the overriding problem from the British point of view was that the military experience of almost all the Dutch-Belgian officers had been gained in French service – the fact that they had previously fought for 'the Corsican ogre' rather than against him was, understandably, seen by their allies as highly likely to lead to cowardice or disloyalty and even treason. Such assumptions would profoundly affect events before and during the campaign, and it has influenced the attitude of many historians ever since. The peripheral nature of the Dutch language has meant that the Netherlands has never been able to challenge the British "Myth of Waterloo" which has so successfully concealed its achievement. Blücher's Prussians have been given their due, but, if they are mentioned at all, "the Dutch-Belgians" are often the subject of derision and contempt while, to quote the complaint of a Dutch historian at the end of the nineteenth century (whose work appeared only in French), 'only the English were heroic, only they defeated the great emperor, only they overran France'. British pride in the courage of their soldiers on those four June days in 1815 is entirely justified, but it should not involve ignoring or denigrating those who shared in the sacrifice.

At Quatre Bras a Netherlands force, outnumbered by three to one, prevented Marshal Ney from advancing across the strategic crossroad and up 'la grande chaussée' to Brussels hours before Wellington could hope to concentrate the widely scattered forces he had arguably misplaced. It is now generally accepted that the Duke's strategic planning for the campaign was flawed, and the untapped Dutch sources starkly reveal his error; respect, if not veneration, for his tactical genius on the field has prevented a proper study of the very real debt he owed the Netherlanders for saving him from the consequences of his grave miscalculation before the battle of Waterloo even took place. Those few Netherlanders gave their Commander the time he needed to ensure that his final battle could be fought on ground of his own choosing and with a concentrated force.

Detailed analysis of both battles will present a new dimension, and attempt to correct many of the inaccurate assumptions, made both at the time and throughout the vast corpus of English language studies, which illustrate what Richard Holmes has admitted to be the curse of historical research: the 'monolingual' approach. Study of Dutch archives in the original results, for almost the first time, in a full 'multi-lingual approach', presuming to join the recent works by Peter Hofschröer and Andrew Field which give the German and French perspectives. On at least three occasions on the plateau of Mont Saint Jean initiatives by different Netherlands commanders, and courageous action by their troops saved British regiments from annihilation. Most British veterans recorded the truth as they saw it, but in the midst of thundering chaos, when as one of them remarked, 'every moment was a crisis', each man had only, in John Keegan's description, 'a worm's eye view': they could have no knowledge of the reason for the failures of foreign troops which they so often enthusiastically reported, nor of success achieved elsewhere in the field.

The creation of a myth in which the Battle of Waterloo figures as a purely British victory has been so successful that the courage, initiative and resilience of twenty-six thousand Netherlanders has, by accident or design, been concealed. Historians are beginning to look beyond purely national attitudes, and this work continues the process – certainly not by undermining British achievement, but by acknowledging at last the long-maligned Netherlanders.

Prologue – the Duchess of Richmond's Ball

The Duke of Wellington planned to host a grand ball in Brussels on 21 June 1815, carefully timed to allow recovery before the rumoured invasion of France on 25 June. When the Duchess of Richmond inquired of him if she should give her own on 15 June, he graciously granted permission, 'Duchess you may give your ball with the greatest safety, without fear of interruption'. Thus reassured by the Commander in Chief of the Allied Army who, of course, would be far more reliable than some of his staff officers who seemed nervous and tense, the Duchess began her preparations.

She was cordially disliked by most people for her arrogance and 'acidity of temper'. Her husband, formerly a lively young man, a demon on the cricket pitch and the victor in at least two duels, had found marriage and the fourteen children it gave him, somewhat debilitating, and had become 'a Gloomy Melancholic Person'. His attempt to cheer himself up had come to an abrupt end when a servant mistakenly delivered a loving message to his mistress to the Duchess instead. She was deeply resentful of the fact that the house he had rented for them was in the southern lower town some distance from the fashionable centre, and had actually belonged to someone in trade – a coachbuilder.

However, it was a large house and the adjoining workshop provided a spacious setting, which she proceeded to transform at a price that horrified her impoverished husband. She hung rose-trellis wallpaper and wreathed the dividing pillars with ribbons and flowers. The markets of Brussels had yielded rich silks and brocades of crimson and gold which were looped and swathed over possible imperfections, banks of roses and lilies perfumed the air and hundreds of candles flared from chandeliers to illuminate the scene.

By midnight on 15 June the Duke of Wellington, as guest of honour, had still not arrived, though the room was crowded with the cream of aristocratic society, officers of the Allied Army in their dashing uniforms as well as many eminent foreigners. The latter were especially impressed with the entertainment the Duchess had provided – of Scottish descent herself, her request that sergeants of the 92nd Foot should dance for her guests, had been willingly agreed to. The men marched in to the sound of the pipes, their full Highland dress shown to great advantage during the strathspeys and reels, and they ended with the sword-dance, traditional before battle.

To great acclaim, they swung away back to their units, and it was noted with surprise that many of the scarlet-clad officers had also slipped away. The band struck up a waltz, but no one danced. The music faltered, people fell silent and into that silence came a strange sound, very faint at first – the sound which has been likened to a swarm of bees – that of marching men.

Marshal Ney, Prince of Moscow, at the head of the left wing of the French Army, entered the outskirts of Brussels....

Could it have happened? Many historians, from Elizabeth Longford to Andrew Field, have certainly accepted the possibility. Wellington's army was scattered over most of southern Belgium, no British unit was anywhere near the main road to Brussels from Charleroi – the latter town taken by Napoleon that very morning in a manoeuvre the Duke had considered a feint. His absence from the Duchess's Ball until after midnight was due to his dawning realisation that he had been 'humbugged'. All depends on the timings – these have been argued over and contradicted through the years, but it is possible to disentangle a thread of possibility even by making generous allowances of an hour or so each way.

Early on the afternoon of 15 June Bernard of Saxe-Weimar, commanding five thousand men of the Regiment Oranien-Nassau (the personal troops of the King of the Netherlands) received alarming reports of the French advance from Charleroi. He marched south from his base at Genappe towards a sound of gunfire and took up position at Quatre Bras where the main road south to north crossed the one northwest to south-east – from Nivelles to Sombreffe. Leaving Genappe soon after five, he would have covered the four kilometres of good paved road in under an hour and he established a defensive position.

Two Nassau battalions, one of artillery and one of infantry had been based at Frasnes, fifteen kilometres north of Charleroi and five kilometres south of Quatre Bras. Theirs was the gunfire Saxe-Weimar had heard as they engaged two thousand French lancers, sent up by Ney as skirmishers ahead of the main force. They were driven out of Frasnes back up the road north, still delivering 'significant fire', which slowed the cavalry advance. Napoleon had ordered Ney that morning to march on Quatre Bras, and the Marshal moved up to survey the position. The Nassauers had concealed themselves in woodland to the right of the crossroads, and in the village buildings themselves, further masked by fields of rye as high as a man, Ney convinced himself that they might be concealing the whole of Wellington's army and he uncharacteristically withdrew. The impetuous Ney of old might have risked it, swept into attack in the hours of daylight left to him, and, since he outnumbered the opposing force by at least three to one, the French could have taken Quatre Bras by 6.30 at the latest; without the Nassauer action at Frasnes (and an earlier one before that against Prussian outposts) they could have been through the crossroads at least an hour before Saxe-Weimar had arrived.

The road north to Brussels from Quatre Bras was one of the best in Belgium – paved and well maintained even where it ran through the Forĕt de Soignies (where its extra width impressed observers) and measured thirty kilometres to the city centre. An infantry division would travel on average at five kilometres an hour on a good road – with high morale and the impetuous Ney at their head perhaps more, once darkness came perhaps less. Night marches were not unusual: sunset in mid-June would be after nine, the weather that night was fine and cloudless, ensuring moonlight despite full darkness soon after eleven. Wellington rode in leisurely fashion with his staff the opposite way from Brussels to Quatre Bras in about two and a half hours the next morning, but, more to the point, the withdrawal of about a third of the Allied Army from Quatre Bras to Mont Saint Jean – half-way to Brussels – on 17 June (partly in appalling weather) took little more. So a timing of six hours is, at least, an arguable and intriguing hypothesis.

It could have happened: the Duke of Wellington's glorious military career might have ended with him trapped in a city crammed with civilians as his army, at that time still scattered over sixty kilometres of Belgium, retreated to the coast, and the small village of Waterloo, instead of bearing a name which entered myth and legend, would have remained in quiet obscurity.

CHAPTER I

The Netherlands

NEDERLAND – literally 'low country' – refers in 1815 to the newly created monarchy that emerged from the Congress of Vienna, combining Belgium with the formerly titled United Provinces (of which Holland was only one) and incorporating modern day Luxembourg. But the very different histories of the two countries reveal the challenges that the Netherlands army (and thus the Allies) faced when, in March 1815, Napoleon escaped from Elba, landed at Fréjus with a thousand men, and marched to Paris where he regained control of government and army without a shot being fired.

Belgium, (known then as the Southern Netherlands) had long been under Hapsburg control, first from Spain and then from Austria, though there was a history of protest against that rule. Norman Davies points out that the final 'Belgian Revolt' when Emperor Joseph II removed the ancient privileges of the noble estates of Brabant (most of modern Belgium) was an essential component of the French Revolution, occurring as it did at almost the same time in the late 1780s in two neighbouring countries that shared a common language.

British suspicions of Belgian sympathies were understandable; the country had suffered so much foreign domination and political change that their loyalties might well be "thoroughly muddled", leading to military unreliability. After an Austrian army suffered defeat at the hands of the French at Fleurus in 1794, Belgium was overrun by France and remained effectively under French rule until 1814, though the paralysis of the Belgian economy and resentment of conscription for French wars meant that nationalism was never crushed. When Napoleon abdicated for the first time in 1814, Belgium was high on the agenda of the Congress of Vienna, and found itself unceremoniously joined to the neighbouring country – the Northern Netherlands (i.e. the United Provinces) – from which it had always been separated by religion, culture, economics and language.

This new state was to be ruled by a virtually unknown prince of the House of Orange. Napoleon himself commented: 'All reasonable persons pronounce this to be madness'. It was the usual story of diplomats redrawing maps and creating new nations to safeguard their own interests, the key here being the security of the port of Antwerp. Antwerp's strategic significance lay in its geographical position in the age of sail. Prevailing winds and currents could drive an invasion fleet directly to the Thames estuary, and, in addition, could enable whoever held Antwerp easily to challenge English Channel shipping. From the mid-1790s French control of the Low Countries had made Antwerp in the words of William Pitt, 'a pistol' aiming at the heart of London, and at last British diplomats had the opportunity to do something about it. On 1 August 1814 Belgium was joined to Holland, and on 24 August the Belgian army adopted the orange cockade as part of their uniform, although formal military amalgamation would take another six months of careful negotiation.

Much would depend on the forty-one year old man whom a patriotic insurrection after the Battle of Leipzig had brought back to his own country's government. The measure of his achievement in providing the Allied Army under Wellington with around twenty-five thousand troops can best be understood by a brief reminder of the troubled history of the United Provinces. The House of Orange-Nassau had known many crises since William the Silent led the Revolt of the seven provinces of the Northern Netherlands from Spanish rule in the late sixteenth century, and established a Republic. Always known in English as 'Holland' this Republic became 'the wonder of seventeenth century Europe'. Yet the fiercely independent seven provinces each retained its own government separately from the federal States-General in The Hague which was chaired by a Stadhouder (or keeper of the State). This post was usually held by the incumbent Prince of Orange, but there was always tension between him and the provinces and, indeed, among the provinces themselves, and the republican enthusiasm of the Dutch never died. In 1650 the future King William III of England was born posthumously and the stadhouderate held by his father was refused him. Twenty-two years later William's military and political genius won him the title as the Republic's economy collapsed and a coalition led by France threatened its borders. His authority held firm after his accession to the English throne in 1688, but when he died childless in 1702, it was argued that since the male line from William the Silent was broken, the stadhouderate must lapse again. The next two Princes of Orange derived their authority from the northern and least powerful of the provinces, and it was not until 1748 that foreign threat led to a popular revolt when a French army crossed the border, announcing that their action was merely a warning to the Dutch to break off relations with England whose Princess Royal, Anne (the daughter of George II) was married to the current Prince of Orange. It was a grave miscalculation on their part – a deputy to the States-General rounded on the French ambassador, 'you're ruining us, you're making a stadhouder'.[1] Anti-French feeling fuelled a revolution that swept Anne's husband to power as Stadhouder Willem IV, and republicanism died for a generation. The fact that his position was for the first time made hereditary seemed to ensure a stable future for the House of Orange, but the mistakes of his ineffectual son, Willem V, encouraged a new wave of opposition through the 1780s.

Pamphlets proclaimed the fact that it was the House of Orange which had suppressed Dutch freedom ever since 1572 when William the Silent had overcome the power of Spain, and newspapers and periodicals fanned the flames of revolt. Local coups all over Holland replaced governmental structures with 'patriot' councils, and Willem V's wife, Princess Wilhelmina, was actually arrested by a Free Corps, or local militia, an action they soon regretted for she was an arrogant and forceful woman with a highly developed sense of her own superiority.

Her arrest was viewed by her brother, the King of Prussia, as an insult to the House of Hohenzollern, and in 1787 he sent an army of twenty-six thousand over the border. The 'patriots' were crushed, but his victory was short-lived: they "never went away" and began to draw strength from the wider Atlantic revolutionary movements beginning in America and continuing in France. By 1795 identification with French ideas of liberation and the abolition of tyranny, and the tide of revolutionary fervour sweeping north from France through Belgium, ensured an extraordinary welcome for another French invading army; it was almost like a carnival 'being happily conducted' as a fleeing British observer reported.[2] In January of that year French cavalry crossed the frozen Rhine, France seized the Dutch fleet while it was imprisoned in the ice of the Zuyder Zee, Willem V was driven into exile in England, and the United Provinces became the Batavian Republic as a satellite state of France, until the year of Willem's death, 1806.

Once Napoleon had declared himself Emperor of the French in 1804, his enthusiasm for revolutionary or republican tendencies was markedly reduced, and he looked for a Dutch regime which would support his own military and economic demands. Still toying with the idea of an invasion of Britain, he needed a totally loyal state at his back, and he abolished the Republic; bronze plaques appeared all over Amsterdam proclaiming 'homage à Napoleon le Grand', and the town hall, through the centuries so often the chief symbol of Dutch resistance to the monarchical principle, became the royal palace of Louis Napoleon, the Emperor's younger brother married to his stepdaughter Hortense.

The marriage was a precarious one (although it produced the later Emperor Napoleon III) but Louis took his role very seriously, immediately trying to master the language of his new subjects. However his first public speech as King went somewhat awry when he confused two similar Dutch words – koning and konijn – and declaimed, 'Mijne heeren, ik ben uwe konijn' (*Gentlemen, I am your rabbit*).

For four years he ruled the country well, beginning the transition from republic to monarchy on which the House of Orange would later be able to build. He also pioneered the strong link between ruler and people by his appearance at scenes of national disaster: when a ship loaded with gunpowder exploded in the central wharf of Leiden, Louis arrived the same evening to coordinate rescue work, help clear the devastation and promise compensation.

Louis's success and independence did not escape his brother's jealous eye since Holland was as important to France as it always had been to England. Napoleon continually chided him for his identification with his subjects, warning that 'a prince who gets a reputation for good nature in the first year of his reign is laughed at in his second'. However, Louis proved him wrong: his insistence that his ministers (mostly provided by Napoleon) should speak Dutch and renounce their French citizenship, his refusal of his brother's demand for Dutch troops to serve in central Europe, and, most of all, his description of the Emperor's continental trade blockade as 'barbaric', while encouraging Dutch merchants to bypass it, brought him a popularity which Napoleon could not tolerate. In 1810 when he realised that Louis was secretly boosting the Dutch economy by such means, he despatched French troops to The Hague. They forced Louis to abdicate, (he was later to suffer mental instability and took no further part in his brother's affairs). Holland was formally absorbed into metropolitan France.

The Dutch army (then numbering around twenty-seven thousand) thus became part of the Grande Armée invading Russia in 1812 and suffered accordingly. The terrible death-toll there is well-documented, but less well-known is the suffering of those taken prisoner by a Russian army totally unprepared for their care. Napoleon tended to use the Dutch troops to defend key strategic points behind his advance so in the chaos of retreat many of these surrendered. If they could prove their nationality, they were better treated than the French but their suffering was still appalling. Sergeant Jan Willem van Wetering had joined the Dutch army at the age of fourteen and had marched and fought all over Europe until he was captured while trying to hold a bridge over the Beresina river. He endured a forced march through deep snow, abused and beaten by his Russian guards, lying 's'nachts in de open lucht ... zonder brand of voedsel' (*at night in the open without fire or food*) existing on a few mouthfuls of raw horsemeat from Cossack ponies;[3] one of only a hundred and fifty survivors from a regiment of nearly three thousand, he would live to fight at Waterloo.

After Napoleon was defeated at the Battle of Leipzig and sent to Elba, the son of Stadhouder Willem V – yet another Willem – returned as Prince-Sovereign and was formally welcomed when a rowing boat launched from a Dutch warship brought him to the dunes at Scheveningen just north of The Hague on 30 November 1813. The print shows the welcome which he certainly received. (Slagtmaand, mentioned in the

Fig. 1: Arrival of Willem I at Scheveningen (Royal Archive, The Hague PR2169)

inscription, is the old Dutch word for November – the month in which beasts were slaughtered for winter food).

The British moved swiftly, sending a small force into the Low Countries to besiege and take their long-time target – Antwerp; its commander, Sir Thomas Graham also brought with him twenty thousand muskets to hand over to the Netherlands army, though he at first refused to do so, judging that Willem's authority was too shaky to take the risk.

Willem moved into the former royal palace of Huis den Bosch and set about laying the foundations of constitutional monarchy. However, such a concept was not entirely acceptable even to those Orangists who had kept the faith through the years, and the republican element in the Dutch psyche would survive well into the twentieth century, surfacing at times of crisis. In addition the ambivalent attitude to France meant that Willem had to tread carefully, while at the same time he was deeply suspicious of Prussian encroachment on Dutch territory along the Meuse.

His portraits reveal a man adopting the fashionable romanticism of the period; the British referred to him in private as "Frog", a nickname perhaps originating with his wide-set eyes and thin lipped mouth. In time he would be referred to as "Old Frog", and his son, the Prince of Orange, occasionally and rather unfairly, as "Young Frog" although he was physically quite unlike his father (he was more usually nicknamed Slender Billy on account of his slight build). Willem was a man of great stubbornness, whose acceptance in 1806 of various sweeteners from Napoleon had in no way reconciled him to exile, and he was excessively protective of his new status. Wellington summed him up in a private letter to London, 'with professions in his mouth of a desire to do anything I suggest, he objects to everything I propose'; while Lord Clancarty described a meeting in which he 'arrived late and was most humble', an attitude which did not last more than a few minutes.

In March 1815, Napoleon's return and the resulting European upheaval offered Willem an opportunity he seized: the Congress of Vienna accepted his proclamation of himself as King of the disparate Netherlands, although this was not formally ratified until 31 May. The Dutch army had accepted the new loyalty and most of that country rallied to the House of Orange as they had done in previous centuries. But the fault-line of the kingdom was there from the start – Belgium was resentful, unconvinced by Willem's stirring invitation of 10 December 1813,

> Wij, broeders, branden van begeerte om uwe pogingen te oversteunen. Bedenkt, ... dat van Groningen tot aan Ostende slechts eene en dezelfde natie woont.
>
> (*We, your brothers, burn with determination to support your endeavours ... Reflect ... that from Groningen to Ostend, there lives now one and the same nation*).[4]

In time of war there might be solidarity but it could not (and would not) last.

There was a third element to be incorporated into the army which Willem needed to establish his new status. Since the sixteenth century the Dutch stadhouders had held lands in Germany as Dukes of Nassau-Weilberg and Nassau-Usingen; these duchies provided troops for the ruling Prince of Orange though during the exile their soldiers had fought over most of Europe under varying commands. German troops were highly thought of, and these had performed well in the Peninsula mostly under French command until, in December 1813, their General, August von Kruse, was ordered 'to manoeuvre over' to the British side. After heavy losses there, many were raw if enthusiastic recruits, and their training was largely accomplished during the march north from the Duchies to Brussels. Their officers, at least, were mostly veterans, but the fact that Nassau had changed sides meant that there would be serious doubts about their loyalty.

These Nassau troops are too often treated by historians as part of the German-speaking element of the Allied Army – the Hanoverians and the King's German Legion – and they were, indeed, German speaking, but since their affiliation was personally to King Willem, they must be treated as Netherlanders and their achievement acknowledged as such. They played a crucial part at Quatre Bras, Hougoumont and also on the left wing at Waterloo, but even recent studies have simply absorbed them with the King's German Legion – the desperate defence of La Haie Sainte owed much to those Nassauers who were transferred by Wellington from Hougoumont for reinforcement, not least because, for once, their supplies of ammunition were adequate – they could have held out for longer.

CHAPTER 2

Creation of the Netherlands Army

ING WILLEM I had a military background, first in defence of his father against the French invasion, and then serving for eight years in the Prussian army, commanding a division at the battle of Auerstadt. He did therefore have some of the experience required for building an army, though it was rather unfortunate that his career had ended in front of an investigating committee accused of the shameful surrender of a key fortress for which he was cashiered. According to the historian, Peter Hofschröer, only the intervention of his brother-in-law, the King of Prussia, saved him from execution,[5] and it was even more unfortunate for Willem that the presiding officer on that committee had been the later Chief of Staff to Blücher in the Waterloo Campaign, August von Gneisenau. There was at least one formal meeting between them which must have been a little stiff, when they met in Brussels for a cavalry review two weeks before Waterloo, but in the months before that, Willem had complained in writing about having to support the Prussians' subsistence once they had crossed his border. Gneisenau rapped back that,

If the King is decidedly of the opinion that [the Prussians'] services are no longer required, they will move [to] where the entrance into France presents none of the impediments … with which the Belgian frontier is crowded.

This was a similar threat to one which the King would later receive from Wellington – if he made trouble, he would be left defenceless.

Willem owed an important element of the army he inherited on his return – one jäger regiment and ten infantry battalions – to his redoubtable mother, that Princess Wilhelmina who had found herself arrested "by the common people" in 1787. From 1812, she had pawned her jewellery and furniture to negotiate loans from Prussian and Dutch banks, and raised the line battalions in both Holland and Prussia; one of them was even partly recruited in Great Yarmouth where she had lived for a time in exile.[6] Willem therefore had a loyal nucleus on which to build as he consolidated his new position. He proceeded on British lines – a regular army, a regular militia and a 'Landstorm' (local militia). At the beginning of 1814 he issued orders for the latter by conscription of all males between 17 and 50, and called on 'alle Nederlandsche ingezetenen actueel nog in Fransche dienst' (*all Netherlanders still in French service*) to return to the 'Vaderland'.[7]

Donations from private citizens were requested as their patriotic duty, and in April 1814 a subsidy of two million pounds from Britain augmented the Dutch treasury which had been almost drained by French demands since 1810 (it was estimated that fourteen million sterling had been extracted from Holland, Flanders and Brabant). The British exchequer had funded the struggle against Napoleon for almost twenty years and the creation of 'the Netherlands' was a purely British initiative. Britain and Holland had been natural allies since the early seventeenth century for strategic as well as diplomatic reasons. As the French retreated, Britain could revert to her age-old policy of using the Low Countries as a barrier against continental threat.

This had been at the forefront of the diplomacy of Lord Castlereagh, the Foreign Secretary: his 'pet project' from 1806 had been the demolition of all French naval establishments in the estuary of the Scheldt leading to Antwerp. A disastrous expedition had been launched in 1809 to capture the marshy island of Walcheren (which controls the Scheldt) and had ended with twenty-three thousand British troops laid low with malaria against only two hundred combat casualties.[8] Disease was not the only problem: the British joint commanders were always at odds – a certain 'Mad Dick Strachan' paired with William Pitt's elder brother, known as 'the late Lord Chatham' on account of his somnolent disposition formed an ineffective combination.

Willem was obviously an enthusiastic supporter of Castlereagh's plans and through the spring of 1814 there was a series of meetings between them in The Hague which laid a foundation for the new state. The Foreign Secretary had been somewhat disturbed on his arrival at Scheveningen to be greeted by a gun salute which turned out to consist of live ammunition; his niece Emma, who was in the party, wrote, 'fortunately they went over our heads instead of through them'.[9] Politely, no explanation was asked for and no reason ever given, but the incident cannot have inspired Castlereagh with much confidence. However, on 18 May Willem minuted:

> Lord Castlereagh commenca par observer que la deliverance de la Hollande, son entire separation d'avec la France et le retablissement de la Maison d'Orange en Hollande etaient des objets qui [ferient] toujours regardés par ce pays (Angleterre).[10]
>
> (*Lord Castlereagh began by observing that the liberation of Holland, her entire separation from France and the revival of the House of Orange and Holland were objectives always to be borne in mind by [his] country.*)

The Duke of Wellington entirely shared Castlereagh's enthusiasm, viewing the Netherlands as 'a bulwark to Europe' and 'a secure communication with England'.[11] The latter conviction was to take precedence over almost everything else in his strategic planning for the Waterloo campaign.

By the spring of 1815 the Netherlands army numbers looked promising, and on Napoleon's return Willem could offer the Allied Army around twenty-five thousand men. This compared favourably with Wellington's purely British contingent – as opposed to the German one – of around twenty-six thousand after almost fifty thousand of his Peninsular campaign veterans had either been disbanded or sent to North America (actual figures are always disputed but the proportions are largely valid). However the Dutch-Belgian quality was suspect on many counts, in logistics, capability and, most important of all, allegiance.

The Netherlands had had less than eighteen months to equip their army. Uniforms had been issued gradually to the new recruits, but there was little consistency, and only the orange cockade was universal.

These uniforms, though of British infantry cut, were dark green for the Nassauers, the Dutch jäger and the Belgian chasseurs; all the rest wore dark blue, only different facings distinguishing them from each other, or, more importantly, from the French – a relevant point for battlefield recognition.

Some new recruits were supplied with M1777 muskets which had been abandoned by the retreating French, others received ones of the British India pattern – the 'Brown Bess' – and these were probably the ones which Graham had brought over from England; one advantage was that since the bore of the Brown Bess was wider than the French, captured ammunition might be used in it, although with less accuracy. However, with factories in Leiden and Delft turning out their own M1815 muskets, such diversity would still cause severe problems – even the nearest supply wagons might not provide the right *matériel*.

Another lack was horse-power; though every citizen had welcomed the chance of selling his riding horses at a good profit, there could be few reserves, and even as late as March 1815 the reviewing general of a Hussar regiment noted in despair that only half the troopers were mounted. The immensely detailed list of requirements submitted to the King itemised eight thousand horses for the cavalry and artillery, two thousand for transport and eight hundred for those generals and officers who could not already provide their own mounts. Most descriptions of the battlefields mention servants behind the lines holding spare horses to replace casualties and exhausted animals, although it is difficult to imagine how they could identify each other in the ever shifting lines. Wellington's dark chestnut charger, Copenhagen, was his mount for twelve hours at Waterloo, but still retained the strength when the Duke dismounted to lash out a vicious kick, (later artists often portrayed the commanders riding grey horses to make identification easier).

For Baron Constant de Rebècque, Willem's Chief of Staff, the greatest logistical difficulty concerned the artillery. By the middle of 1814 the army only possessed twelve bronze English cannon though a hurriedly established factory in The Hague had started production. Six months before Waterloo there were still far too few draft horses for the artillery train, let alone the supply wagons which were often antiquated farm-carts. Many unbroken horses had been commandeered and training time was short; also there was little spare ammunition to test the animals' reactions under fire. Even saddlery and harness was in short supply, the quartermasters were ordered to combine old and new if necessary (rather reminiscent of Wellington's description of a plan of campaign as a head collar of constantly knotted rope).[12] Plans might survive such treatment, but leather was more susceptible to critical stress in the field. Worse still, many of those manning this section had seldom worked with horses before.

In 1816 Colonel Reuther, Inspector of the Army, drew up a report for the King on future army expenditure, based on the mistakes of the Waterloo campaign; in another echo of Wellington – the assessment of his 'infamous army' – Reuther asserted that the artillery support teams had been 'de schuim der natie' (*the scum of the nation*), who had betrayed the forward troops by their incompetence and cowardice,[13] reserve ammunition wagons were found simply abandoned on the road as those in charge of them retreated to Brussels. The final straw had been the fact that 'le jour meme de la bataille de Waterloo le pourvoyeur principal abandonna ses contrats et prit la fuite,' (*on the very day of the battle of Waterloo the principal purveyor reneged on his contracts and fled*); this probably refers to the twelve-pounder batteries which had been withdrawn to Antwerp the night before. The non-integration of the gunners and the supply troops (the British had created the artillery's own Corps of Drivers in 1794) also created difficulty: with neither experience, regimental morale, nor, it must be said, nerve, confusion was inevitable and supply impaired.

An indication of the enormous logistical problem of supply faced by a hastily formed army can be found in a volume published many years later in the series *Ons Leger* (Our Army). For a single artillery battery of six-pounders, the requirements were '6 canons, 12 caissons, 2 howitzers, 46 voertuigen met 244 paarden'. (*6 cannon, 12 ammunition wagons, 2 howitzers, 46 gun-carriages with 244 horses.*)[14] This figure can be quadrupled to reveal the catastrophe caused by that withdrawal to Antwerp. A single cavalry regiment at full strength required four tonnes of fodder a day, and it was estimated that its maintenance alone was equal to that of twelve infantry battalions. Each man was due one and a half pounds of bread, one pound of meat and a little rice and salt per day, transported by the unreliable supply wagons, but even if they received it, an urgent order to march often meant that the cooking pots had to be emptied and the food left behind. Most men would also receive a small measure of genever – alcohol was a separate item, issued from wagons or mules, supervised by women (often wives of men in the field).

Reuther's report reveals what must have been another problem – he specifies that new wagons must have iron axles; since the rainstorm on the night of 17–18 June surprised even Peninsular veterans with its ferocity, many of the wooden-wheeled wagons sank in clinging mud. The central part of "la grande chaussée" was paved, but the jostling chaos of marching infantry, artillery batteries and supply wagons all claiming priority, meant that many were pushed aside into the bordering ditches, or even the fields.

King Willem was probably as doubtful as the Duke about the capability of his troops. He hopefully announced a military decoration with four classes – the Willemsorde, and the cries 'Oranje boven' and 'lang leve Oranje' were incorporated into parade ground disciplines. His army had "evolved" chaotically as recruits and veterans, either Dutch or Belgian, arrived over a period of months with continual changes of uniform, re-numbering of regiments, new amalgamations and adjustments of command. He was at least fortunate in the calibre of his officers; most of them had years of experience in other armies and many key figures returned from French service, though they had to overcome the switch from a glorious Imperial army to what might unkindly be described as 'an operetta one'. There was some disparity among Willem's locally recruited officers: veterans from the 1794 Revolutionary Wars which had sent Willem V into exile, now rallied to his son, though after twenty years of civilian life they might not offer much expertise, and at the opposite extreme, a military academy established in Delft in January 1814 was producing enthusiastic cadets of seventeen and eighteen.

There was little time for training, either in weaponry or in the battle disciplines which would be required, and it was reported that the army's drill was 'the laughing stock of the local civilians', and that its men 'demonstrated an eagerness to desert at every opportunity'.[15] While the latter remark may have been unfair, inadequate parade-ground training might be expected to result in vulnerability under fire. Given time, it was confidently assumed that the battle training would improve, the British subsidy would remedy the lack of equipment, and by the time of the planned invasion of France, all would be well. This was anticipated as a joint operation with the Austrians and Russians whose preparations would not be complete until the beginning of July.

Wellington's most serious miscalculation through May and the early part of June was that he did not expect the French to take the initiative: he (and Castlereagh) assumed that the risk of royalist uprisings and the possibly unstable political situation in Paris would keep Napoleon in France, and, as he assured Castlereagh's half-brother, Charles Stuart, envoy in Den Haag, 'Blücher and I are so well united and so strong' it was unlikely that they would be attacked.[16] On the other hand, his obsessive fear of being surprised still led him to spread his army across southern Belgium guarding every one of the possible routes an invading French army might take. On 16 June at Quatre Bras, this left six thousand five hundred Netherlands infantry with no cavalry support and only sixteen artillery pieces, exposed to a French attack of thirty thousand infantry, three thousand cavalry and sixty-two guns. They were presented with a challenge they were only able to meet at terrible cost.

Blücher shared Wellington's confidence, writing to his wife, 'Bonaparte will not attack us'. However, his Prussians were better placed to guard the 'hinge' between the two armies, since they had gradually moved into Netherlands territory from early May. The two commanders had met at Tirlemont on 3 May to develop their plans, and the Duke was reassured, writing to the Prince of Orange that 'my meeting with Blücher was very satisfactory'. A Bavarian observer at the Prussian headquarters understood that 'in the event of an enemy offensive, the armies would be united'. After that meeting, in a flurry of new orders Blücher moved his headquarters closer to Wellington, II Corps and III Corps were ordered to move closer from Trier and Koblenz to Bastogne and Malmédy and I Corps was ordered to deploy round Charleroi itself – "la grande chaussée" was now protected. However, the Duke's deployment barely changed after Tirlemont – from the end of April, 'the troops of the Low Countries will collect upon Soignies and Braine le Comte' (twenty-five kilometres from the chaussée), 'the British and Hanoverians in the neighbourhood of Enghien', (thirty kilometres from the chaussée). His assertion in a letter to his cavalry commander, Lord Uxbridge, that 'the whole army can be collected in one short movement with the Prussians on our left', took optimism to its limits.

The assumptions of their superiors were certainly questioned at the time by a number of junior officers who felt that they 'had allowed a prudent caution to give way to an unjustified euphoria.'[17] A Prussian officer with experience of three campaigns against Napoleon and one under him, was especially concerned: some years later Colonel von Clausewitz wrote that by the beginning of June,

> One could no longer count with any certainty on receiving a second warning before the outbreak of hostilities, and it was therefore high time to gather forces in greater strength and to dispose them in such a manner that every corps could reach the field of battle in twenty-four hours at the outside.[18]

Even forty hours after the French advance into Belgium, the Allied concentration was still far from complete.

The Duke's miscalculation was closely related to his attitude to the Netherlanders who, in the event, were his main local source of intelligence about French movements. His chief concern, shared by every informed (and uninformed) British source, was a valid one – the question of the loyalty of the sizable Netherlands contingent. The Napoleonic historian, Charles Oman, despite his scorn of the 'Dutch-Belgians', does distinguish between the officers and the men, rating the former as skilled and professional.[19] So, indeed most of them proved, but Oman was writing seventy years later with the benefit of hindsight; in the spring of 1815 apprehension about their loyalty was understandable. The military experience, which was so vital for the men they were to lead, had mostly been gained in French service, and the Prince-Regent himself worried about an army officered by former enemies which might display, 'les memes violations du serment et de l'honneur qui se sont malheureusement manifestées en France.' (*the same violations of oath and honour which show themselves so unfortunately in France*).[20] His concern was increased by the fact that, as Napoleon marched north to Paris, units of the Bourbon army sent to stop him, simply threw in their lot with him. Subversion, if not treason, by the Netherlanders seemed highly likely; after all, the similar uniforms would make it extremely easy to switch sides in the field. The firm convictions of the ordinary British soldier were summed up by the spiteful Frederick Pattison of the 33rd who had little time for foreigners anyway: 'the whole Belgian force has already shown that they would have joyfully placed themselves under his [Napoleon's] standard.'[21]

General David Chassé, commander of the 3rd Dutch-Belgian Division, and Major-General Jean-Baptiste van Merlen, heading a mixed regiment of Belgian Dragoons and Dutch Hussars, had both been created Barons of the Empire by Napoleon, and both held the Légion d'Honneur. Van Merlen and Major-General Charles Etienne Ghingy (also a Baron of the Empire) would actually be required to face French regiments they had recently commanded, while van Merlen's brother remained in French service. The youthful Bernard of Saxe-Weimar had fought for the French at the battle of Wagram and afterwards received the Légion d'Honneur. Ronald Pawly quotes an anonymous report which he describes as 'possibly by Wellington himself':

> All the commanders are known to be French minded [they] are not to be trusted ... why don't they dismiss useless and dangerous elements like General Chassé?[22]

If this was indeed by the Duke, it probably accounts for the fact that he made no mention of Chassé's important role in the defeat of the Imperial Guard in his Dispatches after the battle, ignoring the recommendation of Lord Hill, commander of II Corps, that he should do so. As Hofschröer makes clear, Wellington was certainly capable of maintaining his own reputation,[23] and this omission is central to the argument that the contribution of the Netherlanders was deliberately concealed after the Campaign.

Wellington's assumption about Napoleon's intentions was also being influenced by his contacts inside France. He had served as British Ambassador in Paris from August to December 1814, and had observed the skilful "re-alignment" of Napoleonic loyalists. General Clarke – French by birth of Irish descent – had become Louis XVIII's Minister of War after serving the Emperor in the same office from 1807–14. Clarke had been especially involved with Belgium and Holland when they were imperial provinces, and in lengthy memoranda and correspondence he warned against trusting any officer who had been in French service: the men of the Low Countries could be devious, and undoubtedly Napoleon's charisma would draw them back, just as it had with Marshal Ney, originally sent by Louis XVIII to intercept the ex-emperor's march north (promising to return to Paris with him in an iron cage).

CHAPTER 3

The Armée du Nord

IN MARCH 1815 the Congress of Vienna had been in session for seven months. After the abdication of Napoleon and his exile in March 1814 the sovereigns of the Great Powers had attended a great celebration of the end of the "Revolutionary Wars" in London, and diplomats then moved on to Vienna to study the map of Europe, and draw new lines upon it.

The House of Bourbon had resumed its interrupted reign in France with the return to the throne of the younger brother of the guillotined Louis XVI. Louis XVIII (the intervening title was held to belong to the young boy who had died in the Bastille) had, on his return to Paris, been hailed by the war-weary (and romantic) as Louis le Désiré, (Wellington referred to him as 'a walking sore'). He was not unintelligent and he had had the strength of purpose to refuse a pension from Napoleon in return for renunciation of his rights, but he was nearly sixty, obesity and severe gout rendering him by turns lethargic and irritable, and at all times barely able to walk. He and his advisers set themselves to reversing everything Napoleon had changed and, as the hoped-for economic recovery stalled, disillusion set in and opposition increased – he had been restored by foreign bayonets and there was no national power-base. His treatment of the army was especially resented: he reduced its size, broke up the Imperial Guard into line units and halved their pensions, stripped away the Eagles, reintroduced the Swiss Guards who had always been perceived as mere mercenaries, and bestowed military titles and rewards on his émigré supporters while discharging veterans on half-pay.

The alienation of most of the population meant that Louis had only this army to rely on, and when Napoleon returned, it faced a crisis of conscience. Peacetime soldiering offered few attractions and many of the rank and file were ready to fight under any command: disbanded troops with "neither pursuits to occupy their time nor even prospects to keep up their hopes" rallied to the Eagles with the greatest enthusiasm, welcoming the glorious opportunities Napoleon offered them without reservation. His proclamation had assured them that,

> The eagle with the tricolour will fly from steeple to steeple until it reaches the pinnacles of Notre Dame … honoured by your fellow countrymen … you will say with pride, "yes I was one of them [who] redeemed Paris from its shame"

Among these were veterans who had never swerved from their loyalty to the Emperor and would now serve alongside those who had so recently deserted him for the Bourbons and, on returning to him, could be distrusted as double traitors: "the brotherhood which binds one soldier to another" was lost. General Lefèbvre-Desnouëttes, commander of the Imperial Guard light cavalry, set off with his regiment to join Napoleon; most of them refused to follow him and he eventually arrived in Paris with fewer than thirty men. Napoleon welcomed him, restored his command and reformed the regiment, but his rapport with those troops must have been affected.

For the senior officers, 'the return of the Emperor in 1815 placed us in a cruel alternative between our feelings for him and our duty to our new sovereign'.[24] An even more ominous note was revealed in the later memoir of Colonel Griois of the Guard Horse Artillery,

> I had decided to put all my efforts into this new struggle against the whole of Europe. Yet I blamed the ambition of the emperor who had plunged us into an abyss of pain, and I no longer had such devotion to him …[25]

If feelings such as this were to surface at the height of battle (and perhaps they did) all focus could be lost. Material considerations surfaced as well as moral ones since those who had sworn loyalty to the Bourbons had received awards and promotions in return. Many of them only declared for Napoleon once Louis had actually crossed the French border on 20 March as he fled to Ghent; one officer, summoned to Paris by his regiment, wrote to his brother,

> I think I said to you when I left you that I had no idea whether I was on my way to serve the king or the emperor; you will know now it is the latter.

Louis had, at first, received the news of Napoleon's landing 'with calm dignity ... and imperturbable serenity' according to an admirer. He wrote to Charles-Maurice Talleyrand, his representative in Vienna, that he was quite confident that nothing would come of it, adding the reassuring information that his gout had slightly improved. The government newspaper, the *Moniteur*, agreed, 'this is an act of madness which can be dealt with by a few rural policemen', but as Napoleon marched through France, in an almost triumphal progress, with the army going over to him en masse and garrisons surrendering without a shot being fired, the mood in Paris changed abruptly. A placard appeared, 'From Napoleon to Louis XVIII; there is no need to send me any more soldiers – I have enough'.

Twenty-four hours before the ex-Emperor reached Paris, Louis left with his crown and some diamonds – in the panic his clothes were left behind and, most importantly, the only slippers which could accommodate his swollen and painful feet. In Ghent he set up his court again and settled down to await another restoration. He took the precaution of arranging that every post-horse in the town should be kept for his use in case of further flight.

Many of the Marshals had, with indecent haste, paid homage to the Bourbons: it was, after all, an insurrection of the Marshals which had forced the Emperor's earlier abdication. Some of the original creation of eighteen were too old to take to the field again, some remained true to their oath to the Bourbons and others simply lay low. Napoleon's choice of support staff and field commanders was therefore severely limited: he needed two reliable Marshals – Brune and Suchet – to guard his back, the former to the south and the latter based in the Jura to defend the Swiss passes which might be used by Austria. His brilliant Chief of Staff, Berthier, had recently been found dead after a fall from a high window – either murder by royalist agents, a despairing suicide or, according to the

British, over-indulgence – and the replacement was Jean de Dieu Soult who had lobbied for the post. Although he had been one of the last of the Marshals to declare for the Bourbons, he had served Louis as Minister for War, forcing through the large reductions in the army which had caused so much resentment. He had since proved a determined champion of the royalist regime, and would now, incredibly, be issuing orders to three generals – Vandamme, d'Erlon and Reille – whom he had prosecuted for their part in a coup against the monarchy. Most of the army deeply distrusted him as the Campaign began, more especially since Soult's first reaction to the news of Napoleon's landing in France had actually been, 'this man is nothing but an adventurer, which his final insane act clearly proves'. As the ex-Emperor approached Paris he experienced a sudden conversion. (Soult was to prove an extraordinary political survivor, representing Louis Philippe at Queen Victoria's coronation in 1837.)

Perhaps Napoleon was advertising the fact that he could forgive and forget (which was certainly behind his rehabilitation of Marshal Ney), or, more likely, he simply could not risk leaving a man who had already turned his coat twice in a prominent role, either to hold Paris or command a Corps. Soult was a brilliant field officer – he had fought in the Italian campaign under Marshal Masséna who told Napoleon that 'for judgement and courage he scarcely has a superior', and his long experience of fighting Wellington in Spain would have been much better employed in action; he was quite unsuited to the administrative role and his struggle to communicate Napoleon's (admittedly often ambiguous) orders resulted in misunderstanding and confusion throughout the Campaign.

Marshal Louis-Nicolas Davout would also have been an asset in the field; his III Corps' forced march of sixty miles had saved Napoleon at Austerlitz, and his victory against the Prussians at Auerstadt had given him experience which could have been invaluable in protecting Napoleon's right flank. However, with political stability in France far from certain, Napoleon needed an able, and above all, loyal, subordinate to guard his back in the capital: Davout's integrity was total – he had never sworn the Bourbon oath, and was now created Minister of War and military governor of Paris to ensure that Napoleon had a stable base there.

Emmanuel de Grouchy was appointed to the army's right wing – he was a brilliant cavalry commander but would, for the first time, be required to handle large forces of combined arms. Partly due to Soult's incompetence and Napoleon's often confusing orders, as well as his own inexperience, he was to become a scapegoat for French defeat. The left wing command was the most controversial appointment of all: Ney, Prince of Moscow, who had thrown himself and his six thousand strong force behind Napoleon when he confronted him at Auxerre. Descriptions of him vary between 'bravest of the brave' to 'about as loyal and trustworthy as a polecat'. A French account after the Campaign asserted,

> There subsisted between him and Bonaparte a certain misunder-standing, and a kind of reciprocal distrust, very difficult to fathom, but none the less evident.[26]

In such swift changes of allegiance, commanders were substituted, units amalgamated or reorganised, whole regiments lost their morale, and the French army no longer possessed the self-confidence and sense of purpose which had made it an irresistible force for nearly twenty years. An anonymous general wrote later,

> The soldiers, arriving from all directions knew nothing, they hardly knew their officers, and were not known by them. They had much individual élan but little communal.[27]

In the words of the French historian, Henri Houssaye, the army of 1815 was one eager for war yet without confidence in its leaders. 'Napoleon had never before handled an instrument which was at once so formidable and yet so fragile.'[28]

Although his choice of marshals was so limited and there were also doubts within the ranks of more junior officers, Napoleon could still be confident of his Corps commanders. Honoré Charles Reille of II Corps was a thoroughly reliable disciplined soldier with long experience against Wellington in the Peninsula. Dominique-Joseph Vandamme, a formidable, foul-tempered man with a record of reprimands for looting, was given III Corps: Napoleon was reputed to have said of him that if he was launching a campaign against Lucifer in hell, he would need Vandamme at his back. The command of III Cavalry – the Cuirassiers and Carabiniers – went to Francois Kellerman, who was especially renowned for his ability to reform swiftly after the first charge, and his brilliant leadership had become legendary. A physically small man himself, he could manoeuvre his tall men on their heavy horses (especially bred in Normandy to be capable of carrying three hundred pounds of flesh and metal) into a steel-clad phalanx which carried all before it. All three of these men had served the Emperor loyally since the glory days of Austerlitz.

Many questioned Napoleon's judgment of the Marshals, and wondered how far the ten months of exile had affected him. Outwardly he appeared much the same, if more corpulent, and his speedy response to crisis had been apparent during the escape from Elba. As the square-rigger carrying him and the force of one thousand soldiers, including four hundred Grenadiers, who had been allowed to accompany him to the island, neared the coast, a French warship approached; Napoleon ordered the Guards to remove their bearskins and lie flat on the deck, while he prompted a senior officer to take the initiative, hail the vessel, offer to take any messages to its home port of Genoa and assure them that 'the great man' on Elba was 'wonderfully well'. The mention of Genoa probably accounts for the alarming message which an incredulous Count Metternich, Foreign Minister of Austria, received on the morning of 7 March from that city,

> The English Commissioner, Campbell [British Commissioner to His Highness the Emperor Napoleon, ruler of Elba] has just entered the harbour asking whether anyone has seen Napoleon [!]

Sir Neil Campbell, left on Elba to keep a watching brief, had initially witnessed Napoleon's surprising acceptance of his exile. He had told Campbell in September 1814,

> Henceforth I want to live the life of an ordinary [man] ... my only concern is for this little island. I require nothing more of the world ... than my family, my little house, my cows and my mules.

However by the New Year of 1815 his 'île de repos' had lost its charms, and he was bored despite his enthusiastic seizure of an adjacent uninhabited island which he planned to fortify. Elba was within easy reach of mainland France (Castlereagh had argued against it for precisely that reason, but the only alternative offered was English exile). Travellers and secret agents frequently visited the island, bringing Napoleon news of discontent with the Bourbons; on a more personal level, Louis XVIII's stupid refusal to pay the annual income of two million francs which had been promised him by the Treaty of Paris, threatened his very well being. He began to dream again. On 16 February Campbell left Elba for an assignation with his Italian mistress in Livorno, and ten days later the square-rigger set sail.

The shattering news that Napoleon was on the loose again concentrated minds in Vienna. Austrian hospitality had been generous, and the diplomats had been enjoying it to the full; it had taken them all of two months to decide on procedures, let alone the issues for their attention. However, all the decision makers – the Tsar, the Emperor of Austria, the King of Prussia and Wellington himself representing Castlereagh – were now present in the city, and, in Metternich's words, 'War was decided in less than an hour'; a document signed by all declared,

> Napoleon Bonaparte, by again appearing in France with projects of confusion and disorder, has placed himself beyond the protection of the law and rendered himself subject to public vengeance.

Bonaparte 'the disturber of all the great as well as of all the little folks of this lower world', as Colonel Sir Augustus Frazer termed him, had returned, and all was to do again. It was now for Wellington 'to save the world'.

Those closest to the ex- Emperor on the march north and once he arrived in Paris, noted his stiff movement, waxy pallor and frequent abstraction. At the age of forty-six his energy, focus and clarity of mind were probably reduced: the support of his commanders would be crucial, and, as explained, some of them were not really qualified for the positions they held. However, his army numbered around one hundred and twenty-two thousand as against the Allied ninety-thousand and Prussia's one hundred and seventeen thousand and, crucially, it was for the first time a totally French one once the foreign troops he had previously relied on had returned to their national loyalties. It is also significant that this new army contained no militia element – most were regular troops with experience to back their enthusiasm. In a deliberate attempt to assert his renewed authority, he organised a ceremony and military parade on the

Champ de Mars – scene less than a year before of the Bourbon military review celebrating the Royalist triumph. Salvos from six hundred cannon shook the city, drums rolled, and patriotic cheers of "Vive l'Empereur" were whipped up from the crowd, but Napoleon had made a catastrophic misjudgement: instead of a simple chasseurs' uniform or even his familiar grey overcoat, he appeared in his coronation robes from 1804 – violet embroidered cloak, crimson velvet tunic and plumed hat. Since it had been modelled on the state dress of the *ancien regime*, it hardly chimed with his proclamation of a new more enlightened constitution. Civilian spectators were shocked and mainly silent, though he still received an enthusiastic reception from the troops as he distributed bronze eagles to every regiment and received their oaths of loyalty.

Wellington shrewdly remarked, when asked if he expected any French desertions,

> not upon a man from a colonel to the private in a regiment both inclusive. We may pick up a marshal or two perhaps; but not worth a damn.[29]

The only deserter was General de Bourmont who, as one of Ney's A.D.C.s had argued fiercely with his chief at Auxerre. He left a note to explain he wanted no part in establishing 'a bloody despotism in France that would lead to the downfall of the country'.

CHAPTER 4

Coalition

THE WATERLOO CAMPAIGN is at last starting to be recognised as a coalition, not a solely British, victory, and the recent anniversary celebrations have served to emphasise the fact. This book fully examines the role of the almost-forgotten third of the Allied Army. The Prussian contribution is identified as 'most decisive' in Wellington's first dispatch, in which he attributes 'the successful result of this arduous day to the cordial and timely [Prussian] assistance', but circumstances soon conspired to undermine such acknowledgement. The dictionary definition of "coalition" is "an alliance for combined activity on a temporary basis", and common cause with the Prussians certainly proved temporary, soon disintegrating into political rivalry.

By 1815 the term was a familiar one, usually in a political sense, although William Eden, an M.P. and minister in successive governments, had remarked, 'I am sick of coalitions, royal, military or ministerial'. The Duke of Wellington might have agreed since he had been subject to coalitions for most of his life. As Hew Davies has pointed out, political considerations influenced him throughout his career – he could never act as a military man alone, but was always subject to a control from London which might well be contrary to the military aims he was required to achieve. He had always to look beyond the next battle to Britain's long-term political and diplomatic future, and broker alliances and coalitions with that future in mind. Davies sums him up, not as military genius alone, but 'a political general of the highest calibre'.

Another definition for "coalition" might be "accommodation" in the sense which he himself identified in a letter to the British Minister in Lisbon in 1809,

> Half the business of the World, particularly that of our Country, is done by accommodation and by the parties understanding each other. But when rights are claimed, they must be resisted if there are no grounds for them[30]

Elizabeth Longford writes of this belief in "accommodation" as typical of Wellington's pragmatic mind – 'the English taste for improvisation and flexibility' – which would serve him well throughout his military career, although perhaps not beyond. His efforts to "understand" the other party, maintain an alliance despite the inevitable pressures on it, and yet resist capitulation to those pressures, represents an important element in his military career.

In 1796 the then Colonel Arthur Wesley in command of the 33rd Regiment of Foot embarked at Portsmouth for the six-month voyage to India. On arrival he had his first experience of the frailty of coalitions. Back in Europe Spain had unexpectedly detached itself from the anti-French coalition against Bonaparte, and when this news finally reached Calcutta his regiment was sent off to reconnoitre an attack on the Philippines and wrest it from Spanish control, only to be recalled before they reached Penang.

During the next eight years the widely scattered trading posts of the powerful East India Company were absorbed into an area of British governmental control extending from the southernmost tip of the sub-continent north to Hyderabad and in the east into a four hundred mile wide strip from Calcutta up to Delhi. This expansion – four-fold in six years – was the joint achievement of two brothers, Arthur the soldier and his elder brother Richard, politician and diplomat who was appointed Governor-General in 1797.

As commander of a comparatively small army pursuing a policy of expansionism, Wellington's experience in India laid the foundation for the rest of his career. The many princely states formed a microcosm of the system he would later have to operate in Europe; the ambitions and objectives of their rulers had to be understood and respected with tact and patience. Many of them maintained sizable armies of their own (often trained by French mercenaries), and as these were incorporated into the British army Wellington found himself commanding equal numbers of foreign troops – here, sepoys and native cavalry – alongside his own men. Such would be his experience throughout his military career.

His success in negotiating with the princes was noted back in Europe by Gneisenau, at that time a military theorist, later King Willem's nemesis and Blücher's deputy at Waterloo. Gneisenau's early experience in action was in British pay against the rebel American colonists, but he afterwards joined the Prussian army where he rose quickly through the ranks. He never concealed his distrust of the Duke, sending Baron Friedrich von Müffling as liaison officer on Wellington's staff in early 1815, he warned him to be wary,

> because his relations with India, and his experience in negotiating with the shrewd nabobs, have so accustomed this distinguished general to deceit that he has become a master of the art, surpassing in duplicity the nabobs themselves.

After nine exhausting years Major-General Sir Arthur Wellesley left India in the spring of 1805. On his way home he spent a month on the small island of St. Helena, in order to recover from the toll India had taken of his health – he had often been racked by rheumatism, and the violent fevers which had ended the lives of so many Europeans, and he said himself that if he had not left when he did, he could have been permanently affected. A Dutch tombstone in Mysore read,

> Mynheer Gludenstack lies interred here, who intended to have gone home last year.

Unlike Napoleon, who was to describe it as 'a little rock at the end of the world' where 'one cannot see the sun or the moon for the greater part of the year: always rain or fog', Wellington greatly enjoyed St. Helena – 'the most healthy climate I have ever lived in'.

When he landed back in England in September he discovered just how little India mattered in British foreign policy. 'The public mind cannot be brought to attend to an Indian subject', he warned his brother, as Europe was dominated by the newly crowned Emperor Napoleon whose defeat of Austria and Russia at Austerlitz left Britain isolated. Nelson's victory over the French and Spanish at Trafalgar a month later at least gave her command of the seas, ensuring firstly, that Napoleon abandoned his – always unlikely – threat of invasion, and secondly that the British army could launch an attack at any point on the coast of Europe. That accepted, along with the fact that British funds subsidised the war with France, it was clear that Britain would be seeking new allies on the continent.

For the moment, however, Wellesley involved himself in an ill-judged marriage, duty as a Member of Parliament, and, thereafter, secretary of state for Ireland. The dying Prime Minister, William Pitt, reputedly told him that Napoleon could only be checked by a national resistance movement, and predicted that 'Spain would be the place for it': the Iberian Peninsula would be the scene for his next round of coalition-building.

After his European triumphs, Napoleon was pondering new areas of conquest further afield. One option was an invasion of the Ottoman Empire since Austria and Russia were now allies, and another was the Peninsula. Spain was a tempting alternative because of its South American empire, although it would involve "neutralising" Britain's oldest continental ally, Portugal. He opted for the second in what most Napoleonic historians describe as his greatest mistake, even more fateful than his invasion of Russia, and he drastically overplayed his hand.

Spain, nominally still an ally of France, allowed the French to march across its territory to annex Portugal, but Napoleon's treatment of its Bourbon dynasty, replacing it with his brother Joseph as king, caused a countrywide insurrection. Deputations from both Spain and Portugal arrived in London to ask for British assistance against French occupation, and although Joseph's Spain remained an enemy to Britain, George Canning, the Foreign Secretary, seized the opportunity to articulate a familiar foreign policy statement – any part of Europe 'stirring with a determination to oppose France, immediately becomes our ally'. Wellington himself had submitted a memorandum to the government that Napoleon could be drawn into a war of attrition in the Peninsula, and through the next four years over three hundred thousand men and some of the finest Marshals – Soult, Victor, Masséna, Ney, Marmont and Suchet – were indeed diverted to Spain.

The Duke arrived in Lisbon in April 1809 with thirty thousand British troops to liaise with sixteen thousand Portuguese. He issued one of his familiar General Orders – Portugal was a friendly territory and 'its religious prejudices [sic]' should be respected: the British came 'with every sentiment of faith, friendship and honour'. It was an Order often to be repeated through the years as his army showed a regrettable tendency to revert to a horde of looters. The Regent of Portugal had been taken under British protection to Brazil, and one of Napoleon's targets – the Portuguese fleet – safely sheltered in British ports.

Wellington never returned to England during the Peninsular Campaign. The fighting was desperate in often scorching heat and hostile terrain; sieges of towns like Ciudad Rodrigo and Badajoz alternated with the set-piece battles of Talavera and Salamanca. There were failures (at Burgos he suffered more casualties than the enemy, as he would do at Quatre Bras), and victories (the French grip on Spain was finally broken at Vitoria), as he steadily advanced through the Peninsula. Soult retreated through the passes of the Pyrenees in the autumn of 1813 and Wellington followed, instructing his men to leave their greatcoats behind – there would be no retreat through the mountains – and he established his winter headquarters on French soil. The further he advanced, the more difficult his relations with his allies became – the Portuguese fretted about the use of their troops so far from their border, while he was forced to disband many of the Spanish altogether: their commanders had promised them free rein in avenging the long years of French atrocities in Spain, and their brutality was risking a backlash in the relatively acquiescent countryside of south west France.

British military success had been achieved by the incorporation of both Portuguese and Spanish troops, presenting Wellington with the same challenge of command he had experienced in India and would encounter in Belgium. The Spanish, in particular, he found incompetent and ill-disciplined; the chief medical officer, James McGrigor, recorded many of the Duke's private outbursts,

> Lord Wellington declares he has not yet met with any Spanish officer who can be made to comprehend the nature of a military operation. If the Spanish officers had knowledge and vanity like the French, or

> ignorance without vanity like our allies in India, something might be done with them. But they unite the greatest ignorance with the most insolent and intractable vanity.[31]

However such frustration never revealed itself in public. As he himself remarked with perfect truth when there was a question of his recall to a German command before the end of this campaign, only he could ensure success with such difficult allies,

> Nobody would enjoy the same advantage here, and I should be no better than another in Germany. If a British army is to be left in the Peninsula, it is best that I should remain with it.

The enormous strain of this military command was always combined with political considerations. Much of the Iberian Peninsula was governed by local juntas, headed by mayors, landowners and even bishops, so that decisions were taken locally, sometimes in contradiction with each other; there were obvious similarities with the Indian rule of independent princes, and the importance of local allies to an army in unfamiliar territory was to be proved once again. Wellington sent envoys to these juntas to negotiate over access, supplies and support, and, used sparingly, their "guerrillas" were invaluable, if unpredictable, additions to the British army, often encircling segments of French troops by flanking or rear attacks, and isolating them from the main force.

On 12 April 1814 Wellington, in Toulouse, received the news of Napoleon's abdication and exile to Elba, and before the end of the month he was offered the post of Ambassador to France by Castlereagh – he accepted laconically, 'although I have been so long from England ... I feel no objection to another absence in public service'. He spent the summer in London, receiving every tribute an adoring nation could offer him, and then set off for Paris, via the Low Countries where he inspected the border fortresses with the Prince of Orange, King Willem's son, who had been his aide in the Peninsula.

This new diplomatic role involved lavish entertaining – he spent a minor fortune on Sèvres china – and surprisingly amicable meetings with Ney, Masséna and Soult. But his most important achievement was in influencing the Bourbon King (that 'perfect walking sore') to promise the abolition of the slave trade in France within five years. He was straightforward and pragmatic in his dealings,

> He never indulged in that parade of mystification which is generally employed by Ambassadors.[32]

He was less successful in combating the 'paternal anarchy' of Bourbon rule, and resentment against it rebounded on the Duke himself until the government in London actually feared for his personal safety since there were rumours of assassination plots by disbanded soldiers, all, in Longford's phrase, 'Bonapartist to a man'.

Wellington himself was well aware of the danger, 'it is necessary to withdraw me, but all I beg is that it should be done handsomely'. His wish was granted, as he was sent to Vienna to represent Britain in the re-design of post-Napoleonic Europe. Castlereagh, the original British representative, had been summoned back to London where, as Leader of the House, his expertise was needed to counter the determined pressure to repeal Pitt's income tax; this had been originally devised as a war levy and even the concept was being attacked by the opposition in the strongest terms,

> In theory it might be very beautiful to tax every man according to his property, but nothing could be more odious than that a man should be catechised by persons who possess more than inquisitorial powers.

They were also questioning Castlereagh's actions in Vienna. Belgium had been easy – everyone, except the country itself, agreed it should be combined with Holland. Italy, too, would return to being a collection of states, easily dominated by Austria. A so-called Holy Alliance between Russia, Prussia and Austria, brokered by the semi-mystical Tsar Alexander in an effort to base world peace on Christian principles, speedily collapsed when this admirable vision collided with his territorial ambition; this had left a vacuum into which Castlereagh proposed the establishment of an unlikely collaboration between England and France – Bourbon France was not Napoleonic France, he argued, and therefore must be allowed a place in the European balance of power. He could trust Wellington to follow this line since the Duke had already recognised that, the situation of affairs in the world will naturally constitute England and France as arbitrators at the Conference, if those Powers understand [sic] each other.

He had spent the past months ensuring that understanding by his increasing influence with the Bourbons.

When he reached Vienna in late January 1815 the Congress had stirred itself sufficiently after the Christmas festivities to accept the outlines of Castlereagh's proposal, and the Duke's main focus would be on the question of Germany. Prussia wished to annex Saxony and lay claim to the military resources of the northern German states such as Westphalia (formerly a kingdom under Napoleon's brother Jerome). Britain feared the creation of what would later be termed 'a greater Germany' under Prussian control.

The return of Napoleon, six weeks after Wellington's arrival, ensured a speedy resolution of remaining problems. Austria, Prussia and Russia each undertook by treaty to maintain an army of a hundred and fifty thousand men; Britain, having lost most of the Peninsula veterans to North America, had no hope of raising so many, offering a large subsidy instead. However, Wellington was well aware that his Allied Army needed augmentation: troops from the smaller German states would be the answer even though this would bring Britain into conflict with Prussia. He played his hand skilfully, detaching Russia from the Prussian camp by securing the former's acceptance of the need for a German (by which he implied Prussian) corps in the Allied Army. Since he knew Prussians would never consent to serve under him, the only alternative would be troops from those smaller German states which Prussia was seeking to control.

Both sides had their eyes on the army of Saxony – well-equipped and competent; Prussia won them but was then faced with their mutiny. The Duke watched with quiet satisfaction, suggesting blandly that, for fear of further problems, perhaps he himself should take over all the German contingents. A treaty of resolution was finally scrambled through, although it would not be actually ratified until the end of June. Once the matter was settled the Duke was able to turn his mind again to military command and travel to Brussels for his last Campaign.

His largely successful achievement in forging the military coalition to face Napoleon is considered elsewhere, but one last point should be made. A coalition can only work in the context of mutual trust, respect and a common cause: these elements carried the British and Prussians through to victory. The Netherlanders were neither respected nor trusted– the Duke's attitude towards them did not vary from his early conviction that 'those fellows' would form almost a dangerous fifth column in his army; he discounted their accurate intelligence and refused to acknowledge their contribution in the field. Unfortunately, for the rest of his long life, he never intervened to allow them a voice as Waterloo was gradually transformed first into a purely British victory, and after that into national myth.

CHAPTER 5

Language

SINCE FOR ALMOST the first time in the Napoleonic wars the French army of 1815 was a purely national one it might be expected to be even more self-confident and determined. On the other hand, it is not unreasonable to refer to the Allied Army, as Hofschröer does, as 'an unstable cocktail of British, Hanoverians, Dutch, Belgians, Rhinelanders, Westphalians, Prussians and Saxons', and this was yet another challenge for Wellington. The main languages of English, French and German would often split into different dialects which could be understood during training but in the height of battle might easily be confused. A feature of both Quatre Bras and Waterloo was fragmentation under pressure, when troops would often find themselves attached to different units, but courage and morale could suffer if their new commander was not only unfamiliar but issued his orders in a different language. Colonel Henry Hardinge described the Allied Army as 'not unlike a French pack of hounds: pointers, poodles, turnspits, all mixed up together and running in sad confusion'.[33] But at least French hounds would react to the same language.

It is entirely accurate to describe the army, of which Wellington assumed command in April 1815, as 'polyglot'; the English language having been joined by Dutch, Flemish and French, but already German held an important place. After Hanover achieved its independence from France in 1813, there was a hurried organisation of militia and regular troops, and this fledgling inexperienced contingent accepted its former electoral obligation to the English Crown. The Governor of the Electorate, George

III's fourth son, the Duke of Cambridge, warned Wellington about the contingent he was sending,

> The men have been together less than six weeks… they are therefore not in the state of drill I would wish them, the officers for the most part have never served.

The Duke cannot have been impressed, even by the postscript, 'there is the greatest good will in them'.

The King's German Legion was also Hanoverian but of a very different stamp: it consisted of exiles who had left the electorate in 1803 to avoid French affiliation. Welcomed in Britain, it had been maintained in the personal service of George III, and its men were the only foreign troops to receive unqualified praise. By 1815 they were acknowledged to be as professional and reliable as the best British units, and had acquitted themselves well under the Duke in the Peninsula, though their losses there had left them below strength. Their officers were often English, but some contingents still responded to German battle-orders.

Linguistic incomprehension is now accepted as affecting the subsequent perception of Waterloo as the records are filtered through nationalism, if not chauvinism; however there seems hitherto to have been little understanding of what must have been its impact on the campaign itself. The Allied Army's numbers, present on the field in June 1815, divided roughly (figures again can be disputed) as thirty thousand British, thirty-six thousand German and twenty-four thousand Netherlanders. Of the latter, nine thousand were native German speakers (Nassauers), the remainder divided between Dutch (Holland) and French and Flemish (Belgium). To this might even be added Gaelic since some of the Highland regiments might fall back on it in moments of crisis.

The written Flemish language is similar to Dutch, but the intonations, when spoken, are different. There are examples at the height of battle of linguistic misunderstanding or incomprehension which would be attributed to cowardice or even treason. For example, at Quatre Bras the Dutch 27th Jäger were sent to reinforce Colonel Andrew Barnard and his 95th Rifles in the attempt to take the small village of Piraumont – none of the officers could understand each other, and communication by gesture was understandably inadequate under fire.

The Prince of Orange spoke all four major languages: his mother and grandmother were both Prussian, all formal and diplomatic European contact was conducted in French, he spent time in England when his grandfather was driven into exile, and the latter, in hope of his return, would have maintained Dutch as his native language. The Prince's personal correspondence, held in the Koninklijk Huisarchief in The Hague, moves smoothly between the four according to the recipient, and no grammatical errors appear in the written word (often the Achilles heel of even the most fluent speaker) while he would certainly have picked up some Flemish as he took command of the Belgian army in the months before Waterloo. It is possible that his linguistic gifts were as useful to his commander as his military ones. Since the Duke of Wellington spoke only French, neither German nor Dutch, while the limit of Blücher's French was apparently his greeting to Wellington when they met after Waterloo, 'Quelle affaire', it seems probable that the Duke's instruction of 9 May to von Kleist, commanding the nearest Prussian corps on the Upper Rhine, that communication between the Prussian and Allied armies should pass through the Prince of Orange, was due to the Prince's expertise.[34]

The only French speaker at Blücher's headquarters was Graf Hans Karl von Ziethen, commander of I Corps. Astonishingly, according to Hofschröer,[35] Müffling, liaison officer to Wellington, spoke no English, and Henry Hardinge, liaison officer to the Prussians, spoke no German. (The latter must have been anyway somewhat distracted at Waterloo since his left hand had been amputated after being sliced by a sabre while in action with the Prussians at the Battle of Ligny). It seems strange that historians often describe discussions between the two commanders as clear, speedy and direct, when they must at the very least have been protracted by interpretation, and, possibly, ambivalence. The two liaison officers would, in addition, only be able to relay back to their own commanders the information that was issued to them; they had no access to any private contacts or conversations which might have proved useful.

If pre-campaign planning was not difficult enough between polyglot allies, command in the field would be even worse, depending not only on mounted messengers threading their way through the maelstrom, but at some point on interpretation of the orders they carried. The Prince, at least, would have no difficulty in making himself immediately understood to every man on the field, and apparently he did indeed issue his orders 'in alle talen' (*in every language*) since his I Corps consisted of two Dutch-Belgian Divisions (which included the Nassauers), one Division of Hanoverians and King's German Legion and a fourth of British troops. However, the Duke's 'lamination', as Richard Holmes terms it, of the whole army, combining different nationalities within a single Division cannot have helped mutual understanding, even though it made military sense.

The linguistic incompetence of the British was an important factor in their attitude to their allies. Despite being ruled by the House of Hanover for a century, very few people could speak German. An earlier princess of Saxe-Gotha arriving to marry the Prince of Wales in 1736, was assured by her mother that everyone would speak German since they had been ruled by the Hanoverians for twenty years; however, as Lord Hervey remarked in his memoirs, 'I believe there were not three natives in England that understood one word of it'. So on the morning of 16 June when the 92nd Foot met wagons carrying Prussian wounded from their early encounter with the French north of Charleroi, communication was minimal, and the worst conclusions drawn, 'we suspected treachery on the part of the foreigners ... we did not credit much what the Prussians told us', or – probably – understood it.

The overweening confidence of the British in their own racial superiority would be a factor before, during and after the campaign. One veteran spoke approvingly of 'the steady determined look in the clean shaven face of an English soldier which we did not find in the whiskered moustachioed countenance of the foreigners'.[36]

CHAPTER 6

Brussels

A FTER NAPOLEON'S ABDICATION in 1814 King Willem's dual capital of Brussels had become almost an extension of London's social scene. Aristocratic families who had been barred from continental travel for so long flocked to the city, often encouraged by the fact that the cost of living was amazingly cheap – one visitor found Indian silks on sale in one of the markets at half the price they would have been in London. Renting houses in the city and the surrounding countryside the émigrés entertained lavishly with balls, formal dinners and picnics – the latter at attractive local beauty spots such as the chateau of Hougoumont. A gentleman's club (aka gambling hell) and a theatre provided public entertainment, and as spring turned to summer, the central park, with its tall trees, its small lake and its rose-gardens, provided a delightful arena for gossip and flirtation.

As Napoleon advanced towards Paris, many of the British residents there considered a (no doubt) temporary retreat to Brussels preferable to the upheaval of a return to London, and a fresh influx of notables arrived. The Belgians were delighted by such a boost to their economy, and, with every outlying chateau and grand town house rented, Brussels became 'an Anglophone resort'. Social life received a further boost as British troops began to arrive to join the Allied Army – elegant scarlet-coated officers were welcome at every party, while the Highland regiments proved especially popular. The previously decorous race meetings changed radically once the cavalry arrived: Tim Clayton quotes an account of one only a few days before Waterloo at Ninove, where the town's generous hospitality resulted in men of the 10th Hussars first breaking all the crockery and bottles on the tables, then galloping away into the countryside to terrorise any Belgian peasant they met, and finally 'in true Cossack manner' upturning several carriages.[37]

The only concern, for soldiers and civilians alike, through March, was the absence of their military hero, 'Lord Wellington is not yet arrived but is expected every hour and is as much wished for by Foreigners as English'.[38] He finally arrived in the Netherlands to take up his command in early April, and reviewed his 'infamous army' regiment by regiment and troop by troop. Willem's younger son, the eighteen-year-old Prince Frederik, had been commanding contingents in the southern Netherlands. To his relief the great Duke's inspection passed off well with merely a comment that the men were young and very small; Frederik reported triumphantly to his father that 'Hij heeft niet gemopperd en mij ook niet onder arrest geplaatst' (*He did not grumble, neither did he place me under arrest.*)[39]

Wellington's 'laminating' success in the Peninsula had been directed towards using veterans to inspire recruits and the reliable to brace the doubtful, and this was used again.[40] Holmes quotes Sir John Fortescue at some length over the combination within a single Division of Hanoverians and British, or young British and the German Legion, or regular British with Hanoverian militia; however, the Netherlands troops are omitted from this structural explanation. On 15 June the Prince of Orange's I Corps was as described in the last chapter, while the 1st Dutch-Belgian Division formed part of Lord Hill's II Corps which included Hanoverian militias and solid British line battalions. All three Dutch-Belgian Divisions were composed like the British ones, with militia, line and jäger battalions in combination. The cavalry corps, under Lord Uxbridge, likewise combined such regiments as the Life Guards with Dutch and Belgian Carabiniers, Hussars and Light Dragoons.

Political considerations, as well as military ones, were a feature of Wellington's first month in Brussels in April 1815, as the coalition building which had been such a feature of his career, reverted to the military field. Ever jealous of his own status, King Willem stubbornly argued that the Netherlands troops must serve as a separate entity under his own control through the command of his son, the Prince of Orange. This was obviously an unacceptable situation, and at length a veiled threat appeared in the studiously polite exchanges between Wellington and Willem, namely that the Duke might be forced 'to take measures to render it a matter of total indifference ... whether the enemy does or not occupy Bruxelles'.[41] In other words, if he did not get his way Wellington would leave Willem's dual capital exposed and vulnerable. The King finally capitulated at the beginning of May, appointing Wellington Marshal and Commander-in-Chief of the British-Netherlands forces, although operational orders had to be passed through the Prince of Orange or his Chief of Staff, Constant de Rebècque.

The Duke worried about the security of garrisons in the crescent of fortresses – Ostend, Ypres, Tournai and Ath – which had formerly been known as 'the Barrier', acting as a bulwark against French aggression. They had been repaired in recent years to present a formidable defence system (with one notable and surprising exception, that of Charleroi, which would prove nearly fatal to the Allied cause) and since Netherlands' independence they were naturally garrisoned by Willem's troops. Those to the west must now protect Wellington's lines of communication (or possible retreat) and were never far from his mind: in a letter to the government in London, he admitted to fears about 'rascality in the garrisons by the King's revolutionary ministers', who might look elsewhere for help – to France, or even Prussia – in order to rid themselves of monarchy.[42] He pressed Willem forcefully to use 'trusted British and Hanoverian troops' rather than his own,[43] but in this case, at least, his fears were unfounded. The Dutch were certainly looking west for alliance not east: Prussian manoeuvres along the Meuse were closely monitored and Charles Stuart in a report to Castlereagh, of 21 February 1815, assured him that:

> A dread of the encroachment of Prussia, is most thoroughly impressed on the minds of His Royal Highness and of his Ministers. [The Prince-Sovereign] considers [Prussia] to be a mere instrument in the hands of her powerful neighbour. [i.e. Russia, as Wellington had already discovered when he had represented Britain at the Congress of Vienna]

Willem was far too protective of his new-found status to allow any 'revolutionary' ideas to take hold, and there is no indication in the archives that he faced any disagreement. The British were deeply suspicious of the fact that many of the members of his Council for the Belgian provinces were known Bonapartists, but, once again, the King's judgement was justified – they brought experience but not disloyalty to their posts. He did fret that English knowledge of his contacts with Napoleon during his own exile militated against him – the Emperor had given him the prince-bishopric of Fulda and a sizable subsidy when he had established Louis in Holland. However, as Nicolaas Vels Heijn points out, 'welke vorst op het Europese continent had op dit punt een schone lei?' (*which prince on the European continent had, on this point, a clean slate?*)[44]

The considerable disagreement, not to say antagonism, between Britain and Prussia at Vienna during Wellington's presence there which might well have led to lack of trust, meant that it was now vital that the only two armies ready for action should resolve their differences. The argument had accounted for Wellington's delayed arrival in Brussels to assume command of the Allied Army, and it certainly meant that military discussions with the Prussians might be somewhat fraught. It was therefore fortunate that the Duke and Blücher, although completely different in character and temperament, had the greatest respect for each other.

Gebhard von Blücher, seventy-two at the time of Waterloo, was uncouth, virtually illiterate, passionate and patriotic; he was 'a soldier's soldier', inspiring his men in defeat as well as victory. Without his sense of honour and loyalty which drove the Prussians to Wellington's aid, the Battle of Waterloo would have been lost. The Duke described Blücher to the Colonial Secretary, Lord Bathurst, as 'a very fine fellow', and he assured the Whig politician, Thomas Creevey, some weeks before Waterloo, 'I think Blücher and I can do the business'. Creevey had withdrawn to Brussels after a conviction for libel, but Wellington was well aware that everything he told Creevey would be passed on to opposition members of the House of Commons, and certainly used him as a useful conduit. Those politicians were often vocal in their hostility to Castlereagh,

He is proposing to plunge this country into a sea of blood to reinstate the Bourbon line in France... Let the French people settle their own affairs.[45]

During the same conversation Creevey suggested that the Dutch-Belgians seemed to be numerous and would surely be of use: the Duke was contemptuous, 'don't mention those fellows'. His A.D.C., Fitzroy Somerset, shared his opinion,

> the Dutch Belgians are very bad. The new Nassauers show no qualities but speed in retreat and a great respect for cannonballs.

The Netherlanders certainly had an extra challenge ahead of them; those Nassauers were to prove the saviours of Wellington's reputation.

In April another foreign detachment – the Brunswickers – arrived in Brussels. The Duke of Brunswick had been killed at the Battle of Auerstadt, and his duchy absorbed into Jerome Bonaparte's Kingdom of Westphalia. His son raised a new army, formed an alliance with Austria, and then, after yet another defeat at Wagram, he marched his men across northern Germany, and in British Heligoland found a fleet of ships in which he crossed the North Sea, to place himself in the service of the British Crown. He was the uncle of Princess Charlotte since he was the brother of the Prince Regent's detested wife, Caroline, and his grave yet amicable demeanour made him a popular and respected figure in London society. The black uniforms the Duke designed for his men in memory of his father, with a silver skull and crossbones and black horsehair plumes on their shakos, became a familiar sight in the Peninsular Campaign, but after losses there, they were now a young and inexperienced force (few of their sergeants were more than eighteen), and a British veteran was to describe them as 'perfect children'.

Another duty for Wellington in Brussels was the organisation of a British subsidy of six million pounds sterling for the coming campaign (for the Austrians and Russians as well as the British). At his suggestion, Castlereagh turned to the Rothschild brothers – Nathan in London instructed Solomon to travel from Vienna to Brussels, in order to meet 'one of the Lords of the Treasury by request of the Duke of Wellington' to arrange the instalments.

In the Peninsular Campaign the British intelligence system had been masterly, mainly due to the activities of one man – General Colquhoun Grant. Wellington considered 'he was worth a brigade to me'. Grant was a cavalry officer, and often worked in Spain behind the French lines (always wearing his uniform to avoid being shot as a spy). He now had contacts inside France though he was unable to cross the border himself, and he was required to relay reports to his commander through Sir William Dörnberg. Dörnberg was a Hanoverian cavalry officer (later to command a brigade of light dragoons at Waterloo) and was stationed at Mons which was the Allied intelligence centre. His information was conveyed back to Brussels, and also passed via the Prince of Orange, stationed at Braine-le-Comte, to the Prussians east of Charleroi, with, as Clayton has pointed out, French royalist officers at every post to debrief the fairly steady stream of deserters and far more numerous agents.

Dörnberg was the obvious choice for this work since he was, like the Prince of Orange, fluent in French, English and German. He was highly experienced, both as intelligence officer and soldier, far removed from Longford's description of him as 'a witless Hanoverian'. This relates to her examination of his role in assessing the intelligence reports before conveying them to Wellington. He received an important one from Grant which finally confirmed that the French were heading for Charleroi, away from Mons, but knowing that Wellington had already received the information, he passed it on without specifying the source. He had previously told Sir Harry Clinton, commander of the 2nd Division (based at Oudenarde) that the French army was concentrating well to the east, and Clinton had apparently replied, 'Yes, I believe it now, but the Duke, despite being very well informed, does not believe it'.

Wellington's reliance on Grant alone meant that he tended to ignore warnings from any other source, whether they came from the Netherlanders, the Prussians, or even his own commanders like Uxbridge, Hill and Clinton. Dörnberg has borne the blame for Wellington's hesitancy, but there is no indication that he had been warned that information from Grant should rate far above any other intelligence. General Müffling's report in June that the Duke 'believed himself to be very secure on this point', indicates that in addition to Grant he was relying far too heavily on his French contacts in Paris with Clarke and with the Minister of Police, Joseph Fouché. These were almost certainly compromised: there is little doubt that Napoleon was using both men to convey disinformation.

The Duke preserved his usual calm confidence as he played a major part in the social whirl of the English community in Brussels through May and the first two weeks of June. He gave large dinners himself, and was an honoured guest at every ball and salon: he eyed the beautiful young daughters of the expatriate British aristocracy, and paid especial attention to the ravishing Lady Frances Webster, even meeting her according to an interested observer, 'in a green hollow' in the park. His relaxed manner may have been carefully cultivated to calm his compatriots, but, if so, it was to prove a dangerous risk. Rumours continually circulated of French intentions and movements, and people wondered whether to move north to Antwerp, but they were always reassured by the unruffled calm of the Commander-in-Chief. He later spoke of the need 'to tranquilise' civilians, and in that he certainly succeeded. Doubts about the loyalties, the equipment, the professionalism, and perhaps most of all, the integration of his army, probably weighed heavily upon him, but the imminence of hostilities does not seem to have done.

There was, however, deep apprehension in government circles in London: Lord Liverpool wrote to his old friend George Canning on 13 June,

> We have twenty years of political life behind us, but we have never in that time faced a more awful moment than this.

CHAPTER 7

The Netherlands Commanders

APART FROM THE Prince of Orange himself, there were four other commanders who played a vital part in the Allied victory but have been too often unacknowledged in English work. They are Major-General Baron Jean Victor Constant de Rebècque, Quartermaster-General and Chief of Staff; Lieutenant-General Baron Hendrik George de Perponcher Sedinitsky, Commander of the 2nd Dutch-Belgian Division; General Baron David Hendrik Chassé, Commander of the 3rd Dutch-Belgian Division; and Duke (later Prince) Bernard of Saxe-Weimar, who, due to his colonel's incapacity, found himself on 14 June, 1815 in command of the Nassau regiments.

Their names, titles and experience are significant because they reflect contemporary custom in continental Europe whereby many soldiers enrolled in armies other than the ones of their country of birth, and moved between nations as political circumstances dictated. It is not surprising that to British eyes such "allies" could represent a very real threat. They might be referred to as "mercenaries", although the financial implication of that word was not as relevant as it had been in earlier times. These men were professional and dedicated – volunteers who had chosen the military life in which they flourished. It was this professionalism which enabled so many of them to serve through bewildering changes of allegiance as Napoleon reshaped the map of Europe.

But such a concept of loyalty was largely alien to the British. There were foreigners in the British Army at the time – mostly refugees from French invasions – but apart from the valued King's German Legion, they were often viewed in Parliament and elsewhere with some suspicion; in fact most foreign troops were only stationed on the Isle of Wight or the Channel Islands, not the mainland. It was argued that they could be unreliable since they were already traitors to their own country by accepting British service, and so might be inclined to treachery again.

In 1815, therefore, the knowledge that thousands of soldiers in Wellington's Allied Army had previously fought for 'the Corsican ogre', not against him, would influence attitudes on the field, and raise many suspicions of, at best subversion, at worst treachery, and in all cases, cowardice. In addition, the British assumption of the innate inferiority of foreigners was deep-rooted; Barbero describes the nineteenth century English soldier as 'convinced of his own racial superiority',[46] comparing him to modern football supporters. After all, at the Battles of Fontenoy and Val in the 1740s, the Dutch had been the despair of their British allies: they insisted on pitching tents against orders because of bad weather, and, even if they did not flee the field, their lack of discipline caused chaos on occasion as their uncontrollable squadrons of horse either galloped straight across a line of advancing Scots Greys or trampled over two regiments of foot. The newspapers of the day had once reported casualties of over four thousand 'including one Dutchman who was a little bruised in his flight'.[47] Even sixty years on, the dire performance of the Dutch probably lingered in military minds as an unshakable belief.

Baron Constant de Rebècque, 1773–1850

Baron de Rebècque was Swiss by birth. At the age of eighteen he narrowly escaped death when defending Louis XVI as a member of the Swiss Guard at the Tuileries in 1791. After two years in the Dutch army, he joined the exodus as the French occupied Holland and moved to Berlin to serve with Prussia. Here he caught the eye of the exiled stadhouder who, in 1805, appointed him tutor in military science to his grandson, the future Prince of Orange. Despite the twenty years between them it was the beginning of a lifelong friendship as he accompanied the Prince to Christ Church, Oxford (where they were both awarded honorary degrees) and thence in 1811 to join the British army in the Peninsula, when his protégé was appointed aide-de-camp to Wellington in late November of that year. He was able to observe at close quarters the Duke's methods of training and tactical planning, and he fought at Vitoria which was perhaps the highlight of Wellington's strategic career. He was thus well acquainted with many of the British commanders with whom he would serve in the Waterloo campaign – Thomas Picton, Colin Halkett, William Ponsonby and Charles Alten – and he was certainly greatly respected.

He would also have been made well aware of what Holmes describes as the allied commander's reputation as 'a control freak'.[48] When the Duke's greatly valued medical officer, James MacGrigor, set up a different (and indisputably better) method for evacuating the wounded after Salamanca from the one Wellington had laid down, he was subject to a public tongue-lashing: 'As long as you live, sir, never do so again, never do anything without my orders.'[49] Rebècque must have remembered that incident before his crucial decision to deploy at Quatre Bras in direct contravention of the Commander-in-Chief's instructions.

He was recalled to the Netherlands as Chief of Staff for Willem's nascent army on the initiative of the Dowager Princess Wilhelmina, and his staff work ensured that by June 1815 it was fit to fight. Almost single-handedly, he coordinated the scattered regiments, inspired the recruits and organised the logistic programmes. His obvious experience and expertise would have reassured the returning "French" officers, but his duties extended beyond the military logistics. Mindful of the importance Wellington attached to knowledge of the terrain over which he must fight, Rebècque requested access to the British reconnaissance documents relating to Belgium which had been drawn up the previous summer and copied to the King.[50] These specifically referred to the strategically important roads south of Brussels, to 'the holloways' which often flooded in the slightest rain and the many areas of woodland which might proffer protection or danger.

During the Waterloo campaign Rebècque was usually at the Prince's side, but in his dispatches, and in the journal he kept all his life,[51] he makes it clear that, especially in the field, it is the Prince who makes the decisions. Mike Robinson accepts this in his detailed account of Quatre

Bras, throughout describing the Prince's orders as his alone; in any case Rebècque was, for the first crucial hours, away in Nivelles trying to sort out the chaos there as troops converged from all directions through the narrow streets.

Count Perponcher Sedinitsky, 1771–1856

Dutch by birth but with French and Polish ancestry, Perponcher was both diplomat and soldier. He was enrolled as a cadet in the Dutch light dragoon regiment before his appointment as aide-de-camp to Stadhouder Willem V's younger son, Frederik.[52] After French occupation, he moved with the Prince into Austrian service until Frederik's death in 1799. He then joined the British Army, fighting in Egypt from 1800–1801. As chief-of-staff of a light regiment he took part in the ill-fated British expedition to Walcheren, against his own countrymen. Promoted to Colonel, he was posted to the Peninsula, but resigned his British commission when Napoleon threatened to deprive him of his Dutch patrimony. He then became active in political circles and was part of the emissary which invited Willem back as Prince-Sovereign. He returned to military service as the French retreated out of the Low Countries in 1813–14, but was then sent as plenipotentiary to Berlin. In 1815 Willem recalled him to take command of the 2nd Dutch-Belgian Division.

Colonel Friedrich von Gagern, an adjutant on Perponcher's staff, refers to him in a letter of 23 May 1841,[53]

> The following is to remain private, but I think he [Perponcher] held a grudge against Wellington, which dated back to Portugal, and this made his position towards the latter less agreeable than perhaps it ought to have been.[54]

There is no further indication what this might refer to – possibly the Duke took exception to a soldier succumbing to Napoleon's blackmail; but, it may have some relevance to the decisions before Quatre Bras. Von Gagern had served in the Austrian army and had not been in the Peninsula, but his position on the staff might give him access to information which was more than mere gossip.

Baron General David Chassé, 1765–1849

He was born in Tiel in central Holland though his family origins were French-Huguenot. Wellington's recorded suspicions were definitely understandable since he seems in his youth to have been revolutionary by inclination. He joined the Patriots in their opposition to the House of Orange and Willem V, and after fleeing to France was commissioned into the revolutionary army there at a very early stage. After invading the Dutch Republic in the service of France, he then joined the Batavian Republic army under French control, commanding a regiment of light infantry. In 1806 the newly installed King Louis gave him command of the brigade which Napoleon demanded for the Peninsula, and he took part in the guerrilla warfare there for the next four years. He clashed personally with Napoleon over the 1810 annexation of Holland to France and was promptly demoted to serve under Marshal Jean Baptiste Drouet, Count d'Erlon (whom he would face at Waterloo).

Undeterred, he commanded a rearguard action on a pass through the Pyrenees which saved d'Erlon from disaster, and for which he received the Légion d'Honneur. Marshal Jean de Dieu Soult (Chief of Staff at Waterloo) recommended him for promotion, and as Lieutenant-General, Chassé fought the Prussians through 1813–14. Five horses were killed or maimed under him, but he was unscathed, and became known to the French as 'génèral bäionette' because of his fierce preference for close combat. At a crucial point in the battle of Arcis-sur-Aube against the Austrians and Prussians, the French wavered, 'panic began to spread, but General Chassé seized a drum and beat the charge' to restore confidence. Chassé's action at Waterloo which saved the Allies when the battle seemed lost was a similar example of his quick thinking and inspiring action.

One key event from the Peninsular campaign probably convinced King Willem to trust Chassé when he returned to Holland, despite Wellington's doubts. Some members of his brigade had deserted when King Louis was deposed and they found themselves under direct French command for the first time. Despite his own forcibly expressed doubts about the change, Chassé ordered the usual punishment – death – for those who were recaptured: he declared that he had sworn military obedience and 'heeft nog nooit gefaald' (*had never yet failed*).[55] The firing squad wept, but obeyed him.

Bernard of Saxe-Weimar, 1792–1862[56]

The least experienced of the Dutch commanders but his contribution was both wide-ranging and, on many occasions, pivotal. A descendant of one of the great Protestant champions of the Thirty Years War, Bernard was the seventh child of the reigning Duke, and deciding to make his own way in life, he chose a military career. At the age of fourteen he joined the Prussian army where he later saw active service at Auerstadt. After Prussia's defeat he switched to the Saxon army in 1809; in November of that year, when Saxony joined Napoleon, he fought under Marshal Bernadotte at the grim Battle of Wagram against the Austrians, receiving the Légion d'Honneur at the age of seventeen. King Willem's 1814 appeal brought him to the Netherlands and commission as a junior officer in a German-speaking Nassau regiment. One week before Quatre Bras his colonel broke a leg in a riding accident and Bernard found himself in command at the age of twenty-three. He was an immensely tall and powerful man, and had already come to the attention of the Tsar of Russia who had presented him with the magnificent black stallion he rode during the Campaign.

CHAPTER 8

The Prince of Orange

REBÈCQUE, PERPONCHER, Chassé and Saxe-Weimar are – if they are mentioned at all by English historians – given some recognition for their contribution to the Waterloo Campaign, but the Prince of Orange has been almost universally condemned. He is termed an inexperienced youngster, 'a disaster waiting to happen', a man with a highly exaggerated opinion of his own military talents whose shoulder wound in the closing stages of Waterloo meant that the anonymous French skirmisher did Wellington the greatest of favours. Most of the wildly inaccurate assertions about his character and command performance can be attributed to the fact that the Netherlands' archival sources have never been studied. These reveal a very different picture from the, at best lazy and, at worst vicious assumptions in English work.

Two incidents during the Waterloo Campaign are, indeed, described in gleeful detail – the Prince was the guilty commander who sent the 5th King's German Legion battalion to be cut to pieces at La Haie Sainte and, who, at a crucial moment at Quatre Bras, ordered a line deployment instead of a square resulting in fatal confusion.[57] These two very serious accusations will be dealt with in the battle descriptions, but the more general indictment of his inexperience, ineptitude and stupidity is refuted by knowledge of his life before the Campaign.

He was born in 1792 and was three years old when his family were driven into exile, first in England, but for his formative years in Prussia. Contrary to a recent assertion, which might be said to hint at certain assumptions, he was never at Eton.

He was only twenty-three years old at Waterloo, but at a time when cadets sometimes joined regiments at the age of ten (as Chassé did), and might see action at fifteen (Jan van Wetering was fighting at that age in the Tyrol in French service), it could be said that twenty-three was not necessarily a sign of immaturity. The House of Orange had always recognised that military leadership was the key to their power, however reluctant their subjects might sometimes be, and the Prince had been brought up to carry on the family tradition. Tutored by Rebècque, he applied himself from the age of fifteen to forty-two hours of lessons a week 'avec plaisir et avec zèle' (*with pleasure and enthusiasm*).[58] Simultaneously he enrolled in a rigorous Prussian cadet school and at sixteen was commissioned in the Prussian army. Then in June 1811 he received his British commission, and noted in English in his journal: 'I have the honour of wearing for the first time the uniform of the first Army in the World. Hurra, Hurra.'[59]

This is one of the first entries in his Dagboek, or diary, contained in four one-shilling notebooks for the years between 1811 and 1813. Largely

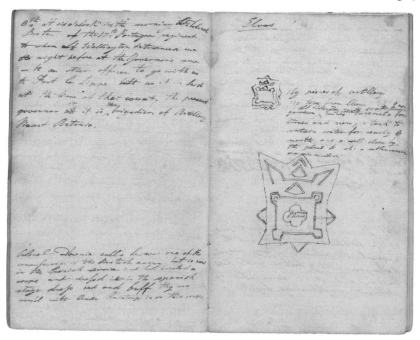

Fig. 2: Prince of Orange's Diary (Royal Archive, The Hague K.H.A., A 40.iv.60). See also Plate 3

in English, it unfortunately peters out when he left the Peninsula. The illustration from this diary shows his sketch of the fortifications of Elvas, the Portuguese border town which temporarily became Wellington's headquarters. Since it commanded the route from Lisbon to Madrid it had been an important garrison since the fourteenth century, but the serious fortifications were actually laid out in the late seventeenth century by a Dutchman (and a Jesuit father at that). The star-shaped defence system, protecting the Governor's house in the citadel of Fort la Lippe, is acknowledged as one of the finest examples of the Dutch system of fortification outside the Low Countries (and is a World Heritage Site today). The Prince's notes refer to the '169 pieces of artillery' and the 'tank to contain water for nearly 8 months'. Elvas also served as a military hospital (and cemetery) for the casualties from the Battle of Albuera and the three sieges of Badajoz.

The reference to meeting 'Colonel Downie' is also interesting – the Prince describes him here as commanding a Spanish corps whom he 'dressed in red and buff' and armed – rather surprisingly – with lances. Wellington's use of the Spanish army had to involve British officers, but in a letter to Lord Liverpool in this context, dated 28 January 1811, the Duke had previously written that Downie had not the control 'to enable him to be of any service with Spanish troops'. British officers 'need to keep themselves in order and in a state of subordination. I know that Downie cannot'.

Two months after joining Wellington in Spain, the Prince was in action for the first time. He was praised for his steadiness and intelligence, and in November 1811 was appointed aide-de-camp to the Duke with the rank of Colonel. There was obviously a political dimension here – British diplomacy never ceased planning for a post-Napoleonic Europe – but Wellington had had ample time to observe him, and the appointment would never have been made without his approval. He demanded the highest standards from his aides, and even political considerations would not have weighed against incompetence. Sly comments, both then and now, about his preference for surrounding himself with young aristocrats, do not affect the fact that he demanded a great deal from them. As Vels Heijn has maintained, this was 'geen functie voor salonjonkers' (*not a post for drawing room aristocrats*), they had to be superb horsemen and calm under fire (for the Duke's command position was always an exposed one and they were posted there to carry messages). On his way with Wellington's congratulations to a regiment after Ciudad Rodrigo, the Prince was grazed by a bullet, and earlier in the same action, he had been one of a small group of volunteers launching a "forlorn hope" attack on the town, and, using his sash as a tourniquet, had tried to save a companion's mangled arm. The aides were also expected to act as his 'eyes and ears', 'om hun chef in te lichten' (*informing their chief*) of everything they noticed, from the morale of the soldiers to the topography of the region.

In June 2012, six months after the aide-de-camp appointment Wellington wrote to the Prince's father, from Prente la Vara, apologising for doing so in English, 'the language in which I can express myself with most facility', and assuring Willem of his great satisfaction with, and respect for the Prince,

> I have tried to be useful to him from this spring, and this motive has acquired additional force as I have become acquainted with him and I feel happy being of use to him in gratifying his desire to obtain a knowledge of his profession.[60]

For the next two years, therefore, Willem was in the closest contact with a commander at the peak of his powers, and undoubtedly watched closely and learned much. An anonymous English soldier had actually written home in April 1812,

> We have carried Badajoz ... the gallant young Prince of Orange has been on the breach in the midst of us cheering and animating our brave fellows. The fire was tremendous but the young hero stood as undaunted as the most veteran soldier.[61]

This third siege of Badajoz was remembered by the veterans as a night of utter horror as ladders were thrown up against the walls and exploding mines and powder barrels rolled from the ramparts ignited the climbing men who then became a charnel bridge for those who followed. Even those who reached the top found themselves blocked by a "roof" of sword-blades chained together and fixed in the stonework. A soldier of the 95th

Rifles wrote of 'such a hail of fire as I shall never forget, nor ever saw before or since',[62] and a sergeant of the Royal Scots admitted, 'the sight even to a soldier was horrible ... fragments of men torn to atoms met your view in every direction'.[63] The first and second attacks had failed, and the Prince had joined his fellow officers as they carried the wounded to the rear – he wrote 'I do not think what I did was praiseworthy ... I would not have been praised had I not been a Prince who finds flattery everywhere.' Since this appears in his private diary there is no reason to dismiss it as a propaganda exercise.

No survivor of Badajoz could be described as ignorant or inexperienced. The town was eventually taken, and there were terrible scenes as the British soldiers took their revenge against the defenders. Drunk on Spanish brandy and firing their weapons at random, they were completely out of control for nearly seventy hours until Wellington chose the Prince to accompany him and rode into the town to restore order. The Duke himself narrowly escaped a stray bullet, and the Prince recorded in his diary: 'the Enormities and plundering committed by our soldiers exceeded description, I found myself obliged to draw my sword against them trying to protect the inhabitants.' Wellington was well aware of the danger which would face him in the town, and would hardly choose as his sole companion an incompetent fool – the experience may well have been the prompt for his letter to Willem two months afterwards.

The Prince returned to London late in 1813 since negotiations were under way for his marriage to Princess Charlotte of Wales. But after receiving a letter from her the following summer, which informed him that 'our engagement is *totally and forever at an end*',[64] he immediately returned to the Netherlands. The letter is both apologetic and affectionate, connecting her rejection to the obvious problem of his English residence after the marriage; admittedly, she might have been aware of his behaviour after Ascot races when, roaring drunk, he returned to London hanging on the back of a coach. This much publicised incident would always influence British attitudes towards him, but was hardly unusual – it certainly seems more harmless than the behaviour of the British Hussars at Ninove.

One month later, in July 1814, he took up his first independent command, based in Brussels, as a general of infantry and Inspector-

General of all arms and of the national militias. Rebècque was responsible for the staff work, but there was no doubt that the leadership of a royal prince was appreciated by the troops, and morale was high. He took his duties very seriously, frequently visiting the strategically important garrisons of the Barrier to encourage as well as inspect their repairs and provisioning. He also controlled the cavalry border patrols which, after Napoleon's return to France, were a vital source of information. In August 1814, on his way to Paris to take up the post of British ambassador, Wellington had summoned the Prince to accompany him on a tour of the border fortresses; as usual the Duke took careful note of the topography of the land over which he rode, and most probably, shared his thoughts with his companion. The forest of Soignies between Mont St Jean and Brussels aroused his particular attention as a possible protective feature. He was confident of the Prince's loyalty at least, paying him the back-handed compliment that 'he [has] no experience in business, particularly in the business of revolution'.[65]

Long before the problems between the Duke and King Willem over army command, the Prince had gracefully relinquished his own claim, writing to the Duke while the latter was still in Vienna: 'I will be happy to give over to you although I can not deny that I would under the present circumstances do so with much reluctance to any body else.'[66] He also allowed his name to be used in the argument. Wellington complained bitterly to Earl Bathurst about the King's attitude and what he termed his 'crotchets':

> Notwithstanding the remonstrances I before made with the Prince's consent against this arrangement [retention of control over the Dutch Belgians] as placing in too great a mass all the youth and treason of the army, he has given me no control ...[67]

The Prince would have queried the Duke's exasperated phrasing, but he fully understood the impossibility of separating the Allied Army into national commands.

Through the early months of 1815, he imposed a rigid discipline on his men, drilling them from early dawn until mid-afternoon; a resentful soldier complained that he prepared for a campaign by filling the hospitals… Our men sometimes fainted, and more frequently, pretended to faint, from heat and fatigue …it became a standing trick …for some old hand to drop as the Prince passed the line. This always had a good effect and we soon marched home.[68]

The 'inept' and 'stupid' youth may have been soft-hearted but he was certainly aware of his command responsibilities. His British experience led him to drill the men in the British two-line system, which, unfortunately, would present them with an even greater challenge at Quatre Bras when they were inadequately supported for over two hours.

His base in the southern Netherlands, near the French border, through the spring of 1815 was an exposed one. According to Longford, Wellington was 'in constant terror of his impetuous young colleague beginning the war before the other Allies were ready'[69] and most other accounts follow her line. Initially, the Prince indeed favoured an attack on France while Napoleon was still establishing his authority there – political instability in Paris could be an opportunity for allied action – and it is significant that Blücher at that time agreed with him. The Duke also assumed that it would be some time before Napoleon dared to leave Paris, but from Vienna he could not judge the situation in southern Belgium. The Prince's intelligence system was well developed: once the ex-emperor's offer of peace was rejected and he was outlawed on 13 March his political authority in France strengthened, and the small Dutch carabinier patrols stationed on the border began submitting alarming reports. One, quoted below, of a speech Napoleon had made to the army, was specific. The Prince was well aware that a successful French advance into the Low Countries would splinter his father's new kingdom, and on 17 March, when he heard that Louis XVIII had fled to Lille, he wrote to the Prussian General von Kleist whose garrison on the Upper Rhine placed him within striking distance:

Je viens d'apprendre par une personne [sic] de la maison du roi … que ce qui fait le plus d'effet sur l'armée est la promesse de les mener en Belgique sans perte de temps.'

(*I have just learned from someone near to the King* [a woman] … *that the greatest effect on the army* [of Napoleon's speech] *was a promise to lead them into Belgium without delay.*)[70]

In view of this the Prince requested Prussian assistance for support if he was attacked before his Commander even arrived in the Low Countries; he was certainly asking the Duke for more muskets, but more likely for defence rather than attack.[71] His assessment is supported by Baron von Müffling in his memoirs where the latter states that the Prince was concerned that he could neither accept battle nor cover Brussels in the face of attack and von Kleist agreed, in that event, to combine both armies 'at two marches distance from the Meuse'.[72] Even some of his critics refer to the Prince's 'quite sensible plans', and it was an early example of the accuracy of the Prince's intelligence system and his own strategic thinking. Wellington misjudged him; Napoleon was indeed planning to strike north as soon as he could, as his newly appointed Minister of Foreign Affairs, Caulaincourt, confided to the Emperor's stepdaughter, Hortense.[73]

However, the Duke remained convinced that Napoleon's authority was still so shaky that he would never dare to leave Paris, and that the campaign would thus consist of a four-pronged advance into France by the Austrian, Russian and Prussian armies as well as his own. He knew that the first two, despite frantic efforts, would not be ready to move until July, and so he continually advised the Prince to move back from the frontier: 'it is easy to move forward, if necessary, but very difficult and disagreeably circumstanced as we are to fall back.'[74] Even after he reached Brussels, this assumption did not change and it led him into a situation which could have been disastrous.

The Prince remained where he was and his cavalry outposts under van Merlen continued to act as a defensive frontline until the start of the Campaign. They were able to be more effective than those of Britain or Prussia: because the latter countries had outlawed Napoleon rather than declaring war on France, their spies were unable to cross the border, while the Dutch – not yet technically a nation-state – could, and probably did, act more freely. They patrolled the whole area from Tournai to Dinant, and their reports meant that the Prince was always far more alert than Wellington proved to be in Brussels.[75] Van Merlen's cavalry captured several French reconnaissance patrols who had crossed the border, but the Duke's orders were that these should be sent back to avoid any violation of French sovereignty; the Prince's frustration was obvious,

I am going to send back the prisoners this morning with a letter to
Count d'Erlon, according to your wishes.

On 7 June Napoleon expelled all foreign ambassadors and sealed off his
frontiers along the rivers Sambre, Rhine and Moselle; it was probably
this sudden cessation of information which prompted the Prince to
make a crucial decision. On 9 June he ordered the Netherlands troops
onto 'verhoogde paraatheid' (*high alert*).[76] Rebècque defined the order
by instructing the men to assemble in full battle order at various points
from dawn to late in the afternoon, and only return to their outlying
billets at night. The artillery train kept teams of horses harnessed to the
wagons from 5 a.m. to 7p.m. every day; turns were taken to cook a meal
so half the contingent was always ready for action while the horses were
regularly changed to keep them rested.[77] Consequently they were prepared
to move immediately when needed – a sharp contrast to the length of time
some British units took to reach the front line. Chassé, who was based
further south and even closer to the border, received similar instructions,
and in addition he rehearsed actual assemblies at divisional level, some
of them at night to cover every eventuality.[78] Possibly some British units
were making similar preparations, but accusations of Dutch-Belgian
incompetence should not stand.

Prince Willem, de Rebcque, Perponcher, Chassé, Saxe-Weimar –
these, then, were the men who, in the Waterloo Campaign, ably served
Wellington and the Allied Army, though there would be little awareness,
let alone acknowledgement, of their achievement.

CHAPTER 9

Strategies

NAPOLEON WAS SUPREMELY confident of victory, and to wait in France until the further threat from the east was unleashed, would be contrary to his every instinct; an invasion of France would destroy the high morale which he was so assiduously fostering. A possible option would be to fight a campaign similar to that of 1814, using a smaller army to manoeuvre and harass any invaders, but the Armée du Nord was far larger than that of 1814, he had always been the master of attack and also a gambler; for his final throw he would accept the risk of political opposition behind him, after all, the best riposte to that was swift military success.

He was assuring the rest of Europe that all he sought was peace – a message to the King of England (which went unanswered) read,

> Let us now put the years of battle behind us, replacing that military rivalry with one striving instead for the advantages of peace, for the holy struggle and happiness of the people.

Simultaneously, at a private dinner, he was heard to remark 'If a nation wants happiness, it must obey orders and keep quiet'. None of his domestic declarations went beyond rhetoric, everything was focussed on preparation for war. Alan Schom blames Wellington for not realising that the major focus of Napoleon's attention was on cavalry – specifically used for attack not defence. At forty-six thousand strong, the cost of this arm absorbed an enormous part of the four hundred million francs which the hapless Finance Minister Martin Charles Gaudin was ordered to provide, (Bourbon economies had cut the budget to two hundred and ninety-eight million.)

Napoleon probably rejected any thought of remaining in Paris at a very early stage, and began to plan the offensive, though he managed to conceal his intentions until the last moment. In this, Joseph Fouché, his Minister of Police, was of great use: another man who throughout a long career of political opportunism, had skilfully maintained a foot in every camp, he was, as Napoleon well knew, now feeding carefully designed information to the royalists and to Wellington. In the last twenty years, he had served the Emperor in every capacity many times, frequently dismissed as 'he neglected no means to make himself serviceable to the party whose success appeared to be imminent', but always restored to favour. His highly efficient spy system made him too useful (and dangerous) to be completely disgraced. While serving Napoleon in the spring of 1815, he was, apparently, assuring Louis' brother, d'Artois, with whom he had long been in contact, that 'if you save the King, I shall save the monarchy'.

Napoleon's intelligence reports and study of the maps indicated a drive into Belgium through that un-repaired fortress of Charleroi and a strike up 'la grande chaussée' to Brussels. If he could take Brussels, the immediate collapse of the coalition was likely, but even if it held, occupation of the city would set up a short line of communication and supply to enable him to deal in turn with the only two armies who were poised for action. It would, in addition, almost certainly mean that Louis XVIII would head once more for English exile.

The British conviction that Belgian troops, especially, would, in crisis, revert to French allegiance was echoed in France: pamphlets were distributed over the border,

> Kom brave belgen, kom tot ons over, ons Keizer zal goed voor u zijn.
> (*Brave Belgians, come over to us and our Emperor will be good to you.*)

The proclamation to the people of Belgium, found in Napoleon's carriage after Waterloo, seems to assume his occupation of the city before a full campaign, inviting them to join his army in repelling 'the barbarians' from their soil. Also, his orders to Ney included a reference to 'dinner in

Fig. 3: The diagrammatic map shows Napoleon's strategic choices, and makes clear the spread of Allied forces on the eve of Quatre Bras. East of "la grande chaussee" the maze of minor roads and the course of the River Dyle (whose many tributaries were in flood after the rain of 17 June) illustrate the difficulties faced by the Prussians on 18 June.

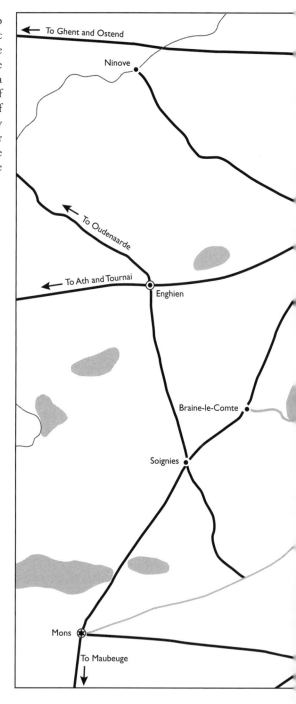

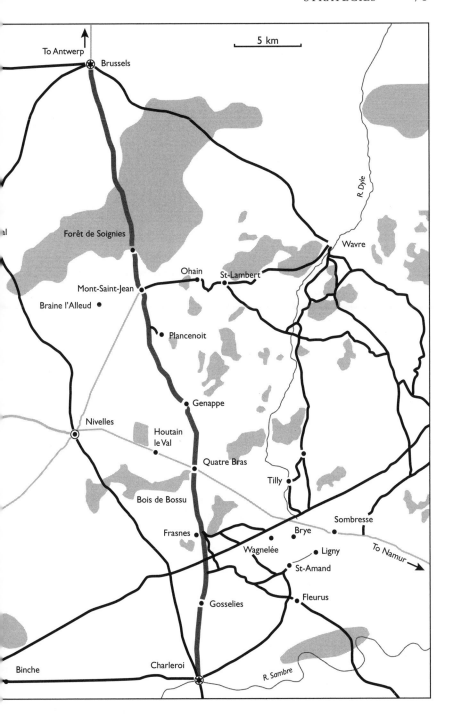

To Antwerp

Brussels

5 km

R. Dyle

Forêt de Soignies

Wavre

Ohain   St-Lambert

Mont-Saint-Jean

Braine l'Alleud

Plancenoit

Genappe

Nivelles

Houtain
le Val

Quatre Bras

Tilly

Bois de Bossu

Sombresse

Frasnes   Brye

Wagnelée   Ligny   To Namur

St-Amand

Gosselies   Fleurus

Binche

Charleroi

R. Sambre

Brussels'. He would have recognised the chaussée as the hinge between those two armies, and seen the strategic significance of Quatre Bras on the road through southern Belgium. Since the French army numbered about one hundred and twenty-two thousand and the British and Prussian combined, over two hundred thousand, allowing them to join forces would be disastrous, but he was confident that he could defeat them separately with his usual speed and surprise, using part of his army to hold one of them while he attacked the other with full force.

A member of Rebècque's staff made the point clearly when he queried later if a mistake had not been committed, 'in assigning as a limit to the two combined Prussian and English armies the most favourable operation line that the enemy could choose if he planned to invade Belgium to take the initiative of the campaign'.[79] One cannot avoid the conclusion that the "mistake" was Wellington's alone; as previously explained, the Prussian deployment placed the bulk of their army at least within reach of the Charleroi-Brussels road, though, to be fair, there would have been no question of a flanking attack to the east.

The village of Quatre Bras consisted of four houses, an inn and three farms scattered to the south of the junction of the south-north Charleroi to Brussels road with the west-east one from Nivelles to Namur. The few paved roads which cut, south to north, through the scattered villages and woodland of southern Belgium were the only possible options for a military attack. Three of these led north from France to Brussels (assumed, correctly, to be the focus for any French attack) – one from Tournai (60 km) and one from Mons (58 km), both of which passed through Hal where Wellington based II Corps to guard against a flanking attack. The third, and most direct, route was from Charleroi through Quatre Bras and Mont Saint Jean (52km). Napoleon kept his opponents guessing through April and May by manoeuvring small contingents of troops on the French border at all three points.

Quite rightly, Wellington's strategic planning took into account the three possibilities, though the route through Mons was always uppermost in his mind, perhaps because that one would, up to the last moment, offer the French the option of the flanking attack he feared. Yet, even so, he was not entirely consistent: the Dutch commander of the garrison at Mons, General Behr, had requested permission to pull down a building which was obscuring his line of vision, and also the bridge over a tributary of the river Sambre. Wellington's expectation of an Allied advance into France (when every bridge would be needed) took surprising precedence over his apprehension, and he dictated a testy refusal to the Prince, forbidding any such destruction, adding, 'foreign officers are too apt to order measures of that kind complained of without necessity'.[80]

Holmes has pointed out that in this campaign, like the one in the Peninsula, Wellington was conducting expeditionary warfare.[81] Just as he had needed his Lisbon base there for supplies and reinforcements, so in the Low Countries he needed Antwerp, and to a lesser extent, Ostend, although there was certainly the option of living off the country during a brief campaign; southern Belgium was a fertile land, where crops of rye, barley and clover supported the stock. The Duke's greatest fear was that Napoleon would encircle him to the west, cutting his supply line to the coast and laying siege to Brussels. Such a movement would also give the French the opportunity to threaten Ghent where Louis XVIII and his court had taken refuge when they left Paris on 20 March. It was a credible calculation in that the Emperor had used such a manoeuvre many times before – at Auerstadt and Friedland for example.[82] The English reconnaissance report in the Koninklijk Archief, requested by Rebècque, certainly studied the possibility of opening the sluices round Oudenarde (as the French had done in 1708 in an effort to dislodge Marlborough).

Against this hypothesis could be set the arguments, most obviously, that it would drive the Allied and Prussian armies together to form a fighting force vastly superior in numbers to his own, and also that Napoleon's more recent preference seemed to be for a full-frontal assault, as at Wagram and Leipzig. The Duke had to be aware of the military reality that he now commanded the remaining core of the British regular army; the road from Brussels to Antwerp might well have to act as a line of retreat in the case of defeat.[83] Unlike Napoleon, he had never been a gambler, he could afford no risks and had to weigh every possibility before he took action; and yet – the most reckless gambler would surely be unlikely to launch even the swiftest flanking attack while leaving two large armies behind him to combine and fall on his rear.

After every allowance has been made, Wellington's miscalculation seems puzzling, to put it no higher. Hindsight is a well-known obstacle to historical understanding, but plenty of his contemporaries were anxious at the time, and only the Duke's reputation as military genius and strict autocrat prevented them from voicing their concerns. Unusually, in the Prussian Army the Chief of Staff (Gneisenau) held dual authority with Blücher and was not merely responsible – as Soult and de Lancey – in the transmission of orders. Wellington would accept no such encroachment on his personal authority, he is on record as saying, 'I did not know what the words "second in command" meant'.[84] Lord Uxbridge, as commander of the Cavalry Corps at Waterloo, and realising that if the Duke was incapacitated he might have to take over, quite reasonably asked Wellington on 17 June about his intentions if the French were to attack first; he received the crushing reply,

> Since Bonaparte has not given me any idea of his projects; and as my plans will depend on his, how can you expect me to tell you what mine are?[85]

He must have been well aware of his plans, and this determination to exclude others from them was characteristic but ill-judged; he was, after all, always in the most exposed position on the field, and, as he later admitted, only 'the finger of providence' saved him. Holmes criticises this 'extraordinary fragility of his style of command'[86] pointing out that he was undermining the ability of any subordinate to assume control: he could have fallen at any time, as Nelson did, and Waterloo would have been no Trafalgar. At the very least, there would have been a temporary collapse as morale was lost and commanders questioned in the chaos who should take overall control – with the struggle so finely poised, a French breakthrough might well have been inevitable.

On his arrival in Brussels in March he had been well aware that Napoleon held the initiative and he recognised that the French had a choice – to wait for an attack on their own soil, or make the pre-emptive strike into the Low Countries. However, through April and May he gradually became more and more confident that the former Emperor would not risk an offensive because it might result in government collapse behind him. The Prussian commander, Prince Blücher endorsed this view, writing to his wife from Belgium in early June, 'we might remain here another year, for Bonaparte will never attack us.' The usually astute Gneisenau was in agreement, he actually wrote on 12 June, 'the danger of attack has almost disappeared'. On 13 June a despatch from Wellington to London reiterated the conviction that his enemy's departure from Paris 'was not likely to be immediate, I think we are too strong for him here,'[87] – Napoleon had left the capital to join his army the day before.

In addition to accepting General Clarke's warnings about the probable disloyalty of ex-French veterans, Wellington maintained close contact with Joseph Fouché. For Fouché, politics was 'simply a double game and its goal was to win'.[88] By May 1815, he was certainly accepted by the royalists as one of them, yet he had made very sure that his republican credentials were not unduly undermined. In daily contact with him after his arrival in Paris, Napoleon was certainly better able to judge his duplicity than Wellington could, but he used him to his own advantage. Conveying to Wellington, on the day Napoleon left Paris, the entire order of battle of the French army, Fouché admitted arranging for its bearer to be obstructed at the border. In Den Haag's Nationaal Archief there is also a carefully written document, dated 10 June, addressed to the Ministère de Guerre (the Dutch War Ministry) from the Duc de Feltre (Clarke) describing the Armée Francaise '500 pièces de canon bien' and fifty thousand infantry under the command of d'Erlon and Reille, though with no mention of the considerable cavalry arm.[89] Clarke, too, was working with both sides, but he and Fouché were so skilful that Wellington could hardly be expected to realise it.

Fouché had continually warned the diplomatic community that a nation which had been 'shaking the universe' for twenty-five years was not going to lapse into tranquillity overnight under any ruler, though his communication with the Bourbons often emphasised the loyalty the royalists still commanded, especially in La Vendée in the west. This latter warning undoubtedly contributed to Wellington's impression, to which he clung for far too long, that the internal state of France was too dangerous for Napoleon to initiate an attack. In his memoirs Fouché claims for himself the responsibility 'for the inexplicable uncertainty of the generalissimo which has surprised everyone and caused much speculation'.[90] It is clear that even within ten years of Waterloo Wellington's strategic hesitancy was being discussed; Fouché did gain an

English translation but generally, as 'the Great Duke' lived on as military hero and revered statesman, comment was muted and restricted to the private memoirs. The troops of the Netherlands were the victims at Quatre Bras of Wellington's "uncertainty", but no criticism of him could be tolerated.

The Netherlands border patrols submitted full reports of French activity through the Prince to Wellington once the latter reached Brussels. On 4 May van Merlen warned that 'un bataillon de 1er Regiment de Ligne' was manoeuvering near to the border between Mauberge, south of Mons.[91] On 11 May an intelligence dispatch from Mons referred to an artillery train to the south where 'men werkt aan een Battery van vijf en viertig pièces' (*men are working on a battery of forty-five pieces*).[92] By the beginning of June it should have been clear that the Armée du Nord was on the march towards Belgium, though much of the information that reached Wellington was confusing as it was combined with the reports of continuing unrest inside France which Fouché was feeding through to the royalists. Wellington also had to consider a further possibility: that the show of force on the border might actually end in a withdrawal. The focus, therefore, shifted to Napoleon himself: if he left Paris and joined his army, then the threat was a real one. Allied intelligence on his movements was generally accurate, and his arrival at Avesnes, twenty kilometres south of the border, on 13 June was duly passed to the Duke from the Prince and Rebècque a day later.

Wellington's reaction to this information is a further illustration of his own wariness, and British doubts generally, about Dutch competence, since he seems to have discounted it, viewing it as a minor disturbance on the border, 'a mere affair of the outposts'. To be fair to the Duke, Blücher agreed, referring to the information he, too, was receiving as 'likely to lead to nothing of importance'. As Vels Heijn comments on Wellington, 'de talloze berichten op 12/13/14 Juni over de concentratie ten oosten van Mauberge schokken hem niet in zijn overtuiging.' (*the countless messages on the 12/13/14 June about the concentration east of Mauberge did not shake his conviction.*)[93] On the morning of 15 June, as Chassé warned Rebècque that the French had crossed the border into Belgium,[94] Major General Godert van der Capellan, King Willem's secretary of state for the southern provinces, wrote to his Ministry of Foreign Affairs that the general opinion in Brussels was that Bonaparte had no serious intention to attack. At the end of the letter he added a postscript:

> J'ai en occasion de voir le Duc de Wellington qui m'a dit en contant de termes "je ne crois pas qu'on nous attaquera, nous sommes trop fort". J'ai apris encore que les dispositions etant telle que dans 6–8 heures son armée peut au besoin etre réunie. Il compte rester ici et attendere.
>
> (*I have had occasion to see the Duke of Wellington who told me in so many words, "I do not believe they will attack us we are too strong". Besides this, I understand that the dispositions are such that if need be the army can be reunited in 6–8 hours. He plans to stay here and wait.*)[95]

This is an important document, and it reveals the Duke's errors in succinct terms: van der Capellan was a careful man who issued meticulous reports back to The Hague, and was unlikely to have misinterpreted what he heard. Wellington's "dispositions" at that time were scattered from north to south over forty-five kilometres and from west to east over fifty-five (initially designed, quite rightly, not only to defend the whole sweep of country from Ostend to Mons, but also to lessen the impact of the army's presence on the civilian population). However, since on good roads an infantry regiment could only move at four or five kilometres an hour and on the bad ones, which ran from west to east, probably at two, the assurance he conveyed to van der Capellan was wildly misleading.

On that same day (15 June) he wrote first to the Tsar discussing general strategy and advising a route through Luxembourg for the Russian army on the eastern border to join him,[96] and, secondly, to Count Metternich about the arrangements for Bourbon officers to garrison the occupied areas of France as Austria advanced. These letters dealing with minor matters concerning the future Allied invasion convey no sense of urgency or alarm. Most surprising of all is another letter of the same date to General Harry Clinton, commander of the 2nd Division of II Corps, about his intention to re-number some divisions,

> Some of the General Officers would wish very much to have the divisions numbered over again, and have their old numbers, which appears a very natural wish …[97]

Such a procedure would, at the very least, cause considerable administrative uncertainty and heap an extra burden on the already struggling staff officers; it is the most telling example of the Duke's confidence that Napoleon would not leave France since Clinton's division was based near Oudenarde, a full fifty kilometres west of Brussels, guarding against precisely the contingency he most feared – the flanking attack. Wellington's defenders have attributed his public demeanour of relaxed confidence to a determined public relations exercise of raising morale, but this mass of correspondence on 15 June would seem to undermine that. The extraordinary miscalculation it illustrates is only now being fully realised, but because of national bias, there has been little recognition of its implication for the Netherland troops whose intelligence had been consistently discounted and who, alone, would have to withstand the initial French attack.

CHAPTER 10

The French Advance

BY THE LATE AFTERNOON of 15 June the Duke knew that the French had crossed the river Sambre, attacked Prussian outposts at Thuin forcing them to retreat to Fleurus, and were menacing Charleroi; but the total obsession with his right flank still led him to suspect that the eastern thrust might be a feint. His own strategic thinking often involved 'a false attack' – at Badajoz he had launched two, ready to follow through whichever one seemed most successful – and perhaps he was crediting Napoleon with a similar idea. In the absence of information specifically linked to Grant, Wellington continued to hesitate. His orders to the army that evening, the first at six p.m., and the second at ten p.m., were still for concentration at various points, not for movement. As he insisted to increasingly anxious colleagues such as Lord Fitzroy Somerset, he was 'waiting for further information before he made a decided movement with any part of his army, it being of the utmost consequence first to ascertain the point to which Bonaparte directed his operations'.[98]

The Netherlands commanders had been far more alert and prepared than Wellington himself, issuing accurate reports of enemy movements, and on the basis of those, preparing for imminent attack. Saxe-Weimar, in a bitter letter to Ernst van Löben-Sels (a military man who collated the reminiscences of veterans in the 1830s and 1840s) refers to 'the blunder of the English general staff who did not know how to gather information about the enemy';[99] this was fair comment, and the Duke should share some of the blame. The Netherlands contribution, and the way in which it was perceived by the commander-in-chief before the Campaign, set the pattern for events during it and afterwards. The Dutch-Belgian troops were the first line of defence on their border with France, manning the garrisons and providing the necessary patrols and intelligence along exactly the line that Napoleon was to target. They served the Allied Army well, or they would have done if their intelligence had been taken seriously. As it was, only the Dutch and Belgian generals reacted to the information received during the first part of June, and their preparations meant that they were now poised to save Wellington from the consequences of his inaction. Perponcher's order of 9 June ordered the 2nd Netherlands Division to be 'ready to march at any moment', every battalion should assemble 'at exactly five a.m. every morning', and if, at seven in the evening, there were no further instructions they could be dismissed, but 'nothing should be left in the cantonments, all the vehicles will be packed, because at the first drumbeat all will have to march leaving nothing behind'.[100]

The contrast with British units is striking. Wellington's retention until the evening of 15 June of an army scattered over hundreds of square kilometres of difficult terrain caused administrative chaos which could have resulted in disaster. The two different sets of orders which he issued four hours apart that night had to be carried through the darkness and unfamiliar byways to many divisions, regiments and companies; sometimes the later orders arrived before the first, many were never received until the next day and there were so few confirmations of receipt that de Lancey's report to Wellington of army dispositions had to be almost pure fantasy, (Hofschröer, through detailed examination, argues that it was exactly that). Even once the orders had been activated the disposition of the troops meant that outlying companies could be forgotten in the general panic. Two veterans whose memoirs have been widely studied, reveal the confusion caused – Ensign Macready of the 30th Foot returned from guard duty to find his regiment had already left, and Cavalié Mercer of the Royal Horse Artillery was more honest than usual when he admitted that he was totally unprepared, 'firstly, all my officers were absent; secondly, all my country wagons were absent and thirdly, a whole division (one third of my troop) were absent at Yseringen.'[101] Mercer waited for breakfast, assembled his troop and set off along the "woodmen's tracks" which served as roads; anxious to move fast he admitted 'the grave error' of separating his columns, moving ahead with the guns and leaving the ammunition and supply wagons behind, which, if he had actually been in action, would have been embarrassing to say the least. In the event it did not matter, since he only arrived when the action was over, in time to criticise 'the cowardly Belgians' in a much quoted description.

Wellington, that evening, was still covering the alternatives of both Mons and Charleroi, unaware that Charleroi had fallen to the Imperial Guard that morning. He feared being caught off balance, though it should be noted that the only troops covering either border section were those of the Netherlands, and there were very few of those. A dangerous gap was opening up at the very intersection of the two armies – a gap which led straight up the high road to Brussels over the crossroad of Quatre Bras; and with that crossroad taken by the French, there could be no swift movement of support from either the main body of the Prussians to the east or the bulk of the Allied Army to the west because of the nature of the terrain.

While Hofschröer's conspiracy theory about a betrayal of the Prussians is irrelevant here, his description of the curious concentration ordered by the Duke on the evening of 15 June cannot be bettered:

> At daybreak on 16 June .... Uxbridge and most of the cavalry [would be] a good sixty km. [from the front], 1st Division over fifty km., 2nd Division a good fifty km., 3rd Division twenty-five km. ...the rest of Hill's troops up to seventy km. and the reserve artillery a good thirty km.

Only the 2nd and 3rd Dutch-Belgian Divisions were anywhere near the likely front and Wellington's order to them was to concentrate at Nivelles (ten kilometres from Quatre Bras). As Hofschröer puts it in his analysis, 'fortunately for the Duke, his Netherlands subordinates were making the right decisions and would plug the gap'.[102] The Prussians had understood, rightly or wrongly, that the Duke had promised to concentrate on his left wing within twenty-two hours of the first cannon shot: as Clayton has pointed out, concentration was far from complete after forty-four hours.[103]

Wellington's complacency was shattered shortly after midnight when the Prince passed to him the message from Rebècque that all was quiet at Mons but the enemy had shown himself in force at Quatre Bras. The original message is in the Koninklijk Huisarchief with a very significant annotation in the Prince's own hand,

'j'ai l'a reçu a Bruxelles, et le Duc ne voulut pas le croire'
(*I received this in Brussels and the Duke did not want [sic] to believe it.*)

The Prince's choice of verb is arresting.[104]

Wellington finally realised that he had been deceived. Napoleon's advance out of France by the western route of Avesnes, the threatening movements round Mons and an initial concentration at Mauberge, had been designed to mislead Wellington and disguise a drive directly to Brussels, dividing the two armies that opposed him. A 'false attack' indeed, but the Duke had read it the wrong way. He was reputedly startled into an unguarded exclamation that he had been 'humbugged';[105] and although he was to insist afterwards that this was by no means the case, his call for a map that evening[106] would seem to suggest that his well-known concentration on knowledge of the terrain had faltered.

Through the rest of the night Brussels was filled with the clamour of drums and bugles as the regiments quartered there prepared for action. The Highlanders gathered in the park as dawn broke before marching out on the southern road, the pipes sounding their pibroch – an invitation to the wolves and ravens: "Come to me and I will give you flesh". Wellington himself snatched a couple of hours' sleep – 'I don't like lying awake, it does no good. I make a point never to lie awake'.

Rebècque had received the news of the fall of Charleroi twelve hours earlier, and correctly deduced that this confirmed the line of Napoleon's main advance since he would hardly have used his élite Imperial Guard for a feint. He had been as conscious as Wellington of the danger of a flanking attack, but he was now able to dismiss the idea long before Wellington did. Rebècque did not have to consult a map to see the danger; he sent an order to Perponcher to station his 1st and 2nd Brigades at or near Quatre Bras itself.[107]

Simultaneously, Bernard of Saxe-Weimar was acting on his own initiative. He commanded a Nassau regiment, consisting of men who had fought well in the Peninsula under Imperial command, and switched to

British service when Napoleon was defeated at Leipzig. It now formed part of the Netherlands force as an independent unit in Perponcher's 2nd Division, and had been cantoned on the extreme left of the British line in the village of Genappe. Through the morning of 15 June Bernard noticed increased movement from the south on the main road, and in mid-afternoon as an officer from the Maréchaussee (Dutch police) panted in to say that the French were past Charleroi, and those on the road were refugees, he heard the cannon fire from the south (against the Prussian outposts) and, realising the danger, used his own initiative and instructed his battalion commanders to concentrate at Quatre Bras immediately:

'Ik ben volstrekt zonder bevelen, maar ik heb nooit gehoord dat men een veldtocht met een terugtocht begint.'

(*Gentlemen, I have been given no orders whatsoever but I have never heard of a campaign which began with a retreat.*)[108]

Due to the previous orders for a state of high alert, he reached Quatre Bras within the hour and joined the 3rd Nassau battalion, whose commander, Major Heckman, had 'through his military instinct' marched to the same place before receiving orders. As they surveyed the ground, a non-commissioned officer came in at full gallop to report the engagement between the French and the Nassauers at Frasnes.

A slight ridge south of the cross-road overlooked fields of rye as tall as a man and very thick woodland – the Bois de Bossu – extended south for over two kilometres parallel to the Charleroi road on its western side. Bernard stationed his men to cover the retreat from Frasnes south of the crossroads where a few scattered farmhouses offered protection. In his letter to Löben Sels, he writes that he was 'advised' – probably by one of the men passed over for the command – to retire to the heights behind Genappe,

I judged Quatre Bras to be of the highest military importance and rejected this advice. You will agree, my dear captain, that if I had followed this suggestion, the battle of Waterloo probably would not have taken place, and you will no doubt acknowledge that fate is often determined by the smallest trinket.[109]

A short time later Red Lancers, having driven back the Nassau force at Frasnes, approached through the wood, and launched a determined advance: they almost reached the crossroads before being stopped by Saxe-Weimar's infantry; a cavalry advance on the eastern side of the road was forced to withdraw by the eight guns of the horse artillery commanded by Captain Adriaan Bijleveld. These efforts were so successful that Ney believing he was up against a considerable element of the allied army, withdrew his far greater force south allowing the Netherlands troops to move forward again. Saxe-Weimar later pointed out that with cavalry support he could have achieved much more,[110] but without his presence he is surely right that the French could have been through Quatre Bras and on the 'great road' to Brussels before Wellington had issued any orders at all. With Ney well able to 'forget' the necessity to maintain contact with the right wing, and anxious for glory, the open road would have offered a tantalising opportunity. As has been explained, the timings do make it just possible for the Duchess of Richmond to have received the whole French left wing at her ball, and with Brussels under French occupation, the scattered army would have had no option but to retreat to the coast as the Duke's glorious military career ended in ignominious defeat.

Ney's contrasting conduct in the Campaign has been noted in the French accounts – at Waterloo he behaved almost manically, leading many of the desperate cavalry charges himself, but at Quatre Bras

> He was indecisive, irresolute in his attacks … This was strange in a man whose audacious determination in war was well known.[111]

The early clashes had already caused the Nassauers some serious casualties, and the artillery had come under direct attack. Despite the loss of thirty horses, Bijleveld managed to get his guns back to Quatre Bras intact, but that loss would be critical the next day when the main battle was expected at dawn. Saxe-Weimar sent a message to Perponcher, warning of 'het risico van Brussel afgesneden te worden' (*the risk that Brussels could be cut off*), and he also spelt out the difficulties which would face the Netherlands troops throughout the campaign:

> Ik moet Uwe Excellentie bekennen dat ik te zwak ben om hier lang te houden…. Mij Jägers hebben geweren van vier verschillende calibres en slechts tien patronen per man.

(I must inform your Excellency that I am too weak to hold out here for long ... the Jägers have carbines of four different calibres and only ten rounds per man.)[112]

Perponcher, appalled, sent the message on to Rebècque, who was facing a desperate quandary of his own.

His commander, the Prince, had left the headquarters at Braine-le-Comte (thirty kilometres west of Quatre Bras) at nine a.m. for Brussels, and when Wellington suggested he stay there for the Duchess of Richmond's Ball that evening, the Prince had accepted. Messages back and forth would take up to four hours, even for the volbloed (thoroughbred) horses used for urgent messages, and certainly longer at night. However, it is a further indication of the Prince's alertness that he left an instruction for his aide,

> to keep himself ready with a fast running horse that whenever news arrived that the enemy had attacked, one of ours was to bring the message with all haste to HRH at Brussels, and another adjutant was to go to the place of the attack to gather the reports and return to headquarters.[113]

He would appear to be expecting the imminent attack, which the Duke was still discounting.

Rebècque's midday instruction for the Quatre Bras deployment had been proved to be entirely correct, but that initiative had been taken in the absence of orders. At ten thirty p.m. orders finally came: 'The Prince of Orange is requested to collect at Nivelles the 2nd and 3rd divisions of the Army of the Low Countries.'[114] A concentration at Nivelles would keep these divisions ten kilometres west of a point which had already seen some hours of heavy fighting, and where the commander obviously felt isolated and anxious – with good cause.

With the Prince dancing in Brussels, Rebècque had to take responsibility. He was well aware of the Duke's treatment of any officer guilty of even the mildest insubordination, let alone direct disobedience. There is a telling comparison here with an event at Waterloo, which will be mentioned later, where strict adherence to orders actually led to a Dutch cavalry brigade having to take action while two British generals 'maintained a masterly inactivity' so as to obey the orders of their Commander-in-Chief.[115] In the end, with considerable moral courage, Rebècque opted in Holmes's words for 'intelligent disobedience', and thereby saved Wellington's reputation. The Allied cause would owe him a very great deal; there can be no doubt that it was his decision alone that maintained the bridge by which the British and Prussian armies were able to link up at Waterloo.

His written orders were couched in euphemistic terms as if from the Prince himself, whom he 'elk ogenblik terugverwacht' (*expected back at any moment*),[116] although they were dictated before midnight and the Prince could not possibly be back in Braine-le-Comte before three a.m. at the earliest. In his final report to King Willem, Rebècque refers to the fact that none of the written orders were timed from that evening onwards (previously this had been meticulously recorded). His journal states that since

> l'ennemi a dèja poupé jusqu'a Quatre Bras, j'ai eu devoir prendre sur moi d'instructer General de Perponcher de soutenir le 2 Brigade avec le premier'.
>
> (*the enemy has already shown himself at Quatre Bras, I have had to take it upon myself to instruct General Perponcher to support his 2nd Brigade with the 1st.*)[117]

He certainly consulted closely with Perponcher – whose rumoured ambivalent opinion of the Duke may have weighed in the balance – before ordering him to Quatre Bras with two battalions. Perponcher's men marched through the night and arrived at dawn, to Saxe-Weimar's relief, having incorporated on the way fifty Silesian Hussars who had been cut off as Prussian outposts south of the River Sambre had been forced to retreat before the advancing French.

Wellington's flawed orders had not even mentioned the Netherlands cavalry. Lieutenant General Baron Jean-Marie Collaert's division was still twenty kilometres southwest of Quatre Bras, to the left of the French advance and in dangerous isolation. Robinson asserts, 'Wellington's staff seemed to have forgotten its existence',[118] and a similar mistake was probably repeated with serious consequences at Waterloo. Rebècque, despite his other concerns, got an order to Collaert by 3 a.m. to march north, back to the headquarters at Braine-le-Comte.

The Prince arrived at Quatre Bras, via Braine-le-Comte, between five and six a.m., having ridden over sixty kilometres through the night, and took command, moving some battalions closer to the enemy, and assuring Saxe-Weimar they 'would soon [sic] be supported by part of the English army'. It was an assumption he must have taken from the Duke himself, similar to one Müffling had passed to Blücher the night before, however the actual time-span would be at least nine hours, (and even then units would be committed piecemeal, many of them exhausted after a long march). The Prince's military enthusiasm led him, rather unwisely, to dismount and lie on the ground to observe the advance he had just ordered. As a French flanking squadron threatened to envelop him, he had a scramble to escape, prompting Saxe-Weimar to refer in a letter to his father to his

> Noble but at the same time unfortunate passion for getting in the way of skirmisher fire.

The defenders numbered just under eight thousand men and sixteen guns, spread over a line of three and a half kilometres, some actually in the Bois de Bossu to give an impression of strength. A line of skirmishers was placed in the tall fields of rye, shielding actual numbers from French reconnaissance. From dawn continuous cavalry probes were driven back over a period of about four hours, and the Prussian hussars, before they returned to their own regiment, showed what Allied cavalry could have achieved. Rebécque's chief of staff, Pieter van Zuijlen wrote of their 'several splendid charges against the enemy cavalry which they pushed back',[119] and the French made no further attempt to exploit their superiority. This quotation reveals two further points: firstly when Wellington arrived at the crossroad around 10 a.m. the French probes had ceased so he saw only a quiet front; and secondly, he mentions seeing 'a squadron of Belgian dragoons'.[120] These must have been the Silesian hussars as the only cavalry on the field, and it is possible that when he and his aides noticed their absence later, 'Belgian desertion' was their natural conclusion.

The inability to distinguish between foreign uniforms in a mixed army is a recurring factor in the campaign, but it would be a very surprising mistake for Wellington to make since all hussars, because of their

Hungarian origin, wore distinctive elaborately braided or laced jackets; on the other hand, both the Silesian hussars and the Belgian dragoons wore green jackets and shakos, and the Prussians, having already been in action during their retreat, might have appeared somewhat dishevelled. It is, anyway, an established fact that no Belgian cavalry reached Quatre Bras until late in the afternoon. Incidentally, this also makes a nonsense of the enduring myth, picked up by Thackeray in *Vanity Fair,* that a fleeing squadron of Dutch-Belgian horsemen galloped back through Brussels, shouting that the French were on their heels. These are identified by Longford as 'the young troops' in the Bois de Bossu, who were certainly not cavalry, while others, curiously, place the incident early the following morning long after Quatre Bras was over. It may be that the confirmed flight of the Cumberland Hussars from Waterloo has somehow been magnified into a mass exodus – any foreign troops seen in Brussels after either battle would be assumed to be deserting – they were 'dastardly Belgians, scampering through the town'.

Wellington blandly congratulated the Prince and Perponcher on their concentrations, and greatly offended Saxe-Weimar, to whom he was introduced by the Prince. Apparently the Duke simply looked him up and down before turning back to the inspection without a word. Years later Saxe-Weimar recalled: 'I was struck by the bad tone the Duke affected, he did not even address a single word to me and turned his back to me.'[121] In this letter (again to Löben-Sels) Saxe–Weimar expresses the resentment felt by so many of the Netherlands veterans as they remembered,

> the wrong and half measures that preceded the outbreak of hostilities, the confusion which characterised the operations …[and] the very little due recognition the Duke of Wellington rendered … about our army during the campaign.

The Duke left Quatre Bras to visit Blücher and Gneisenau, and a conversation took place which has been argued over ever since. All were aware that there would be a decisive battle that day, and that there should be a consultation on tactics; but this meeting, conducted as usual in French, resulted in misunderstanding. Since Wellington had grossly overestimated to them the number of troops he could assemble in time at

Quatre Bras, the Prussians assumed that he would be able to divert one or even two Divisions to join their right wing. He had, after all, assured Müffling that 'a large part [sic]' of his army would be able to concentrate at Quatre Bras that morning. At this meeting he added a caveat that he would join them – 'provided he was not attacked himself'. In the event, of course, Quatre Bras was as "close-run" as Waterloo would be and he had no troops to spare, but Gneisenau's suspicions about British duplicity deepened, and the trail leads back to the Duke's strategic error. However, the Allied army's defence through the day at Quatre Bras did prevent Ney from joining Grouchy in the attack on the Prussians at Ligny as Napoleon intended, just as Ligny ensured that Wellington could hang on at Quatre Bras. The old saw about not dividing an army held good.

Wellington upset the Prussians that morning by criticising their partial deployment on a forward slope. Gneisenau snapped that Prussians were prepared to face their enemies, but Wellington was right: they were arguably lacking, as another critic put it, in tactical finesse. In the battle of Ligny which swayed to and fro over a cluster of villages later that day, the fighting was intense and the Prussians suffered twenty thousand casualties and had to withdraw, thus placing extra pressure on the Allied Army as the French widened the gap between them. A French sergeant of the Imperial Guard later recalled the sight of that long slope, totally exposed to artillery fire,

> A vast number of corpses, both men and horses, were scattered about…. The scene was different from the valley where almost all the dead preserved a human appearance, because canister, musket balls and bayonets were the only instruments of destruction used there. Here, as a contrast, it was limbs and scattered body parts, detached heads, ripped out entrails and disembowelled horses.

CHAPTER 11

The Battle of Quatre Bras

QUATRE BRAS has been, until very recently 'the forgotten battle', overshadowed by the one which followed it two days later. A British veteran wrote:

> Had it not been so closely followed by … Waterloo, perhaps the gallant exploits and unexampled bravery that marked that day would have … excited even more admiration than was actually associated with it.[122]

It is now generally accepted that the narrow victory at Waterloo was made possible by the determined defence of that crossroad which gained Wellington the time to deploy his scattered army on the ridge of Mont Saint Jean. However, the fact that the hopelessly outnumbered defenders were, for a vital two-hour period, Netherlanders has been unacknowledged until very recently. Many men fought in both battles and even for them the defining nature of Waterloo tended to overwhelm the memories of Quatre Bras.

The delay in Ney's advance on 16 June was partly due to the somewhat confusing orders from Marshal Soult, the Chief of Staff, that post 'for which he had relatively little prior experience and unproven ability'.[123] He would find it difficult throughout the campaign to issue orders clearly and unequivocally. But Ney himself was not the man he was: possibly suffering from battle fatigue, he was apathetic that morning, easily persuaded by Reille, commanding II Corps, that the Bois de Bossu might well conceal the major part of the Allied Army, 'it may turn out to be one of these Spanish battles, in which the English never appear until their own time is come.'[124] Ney seems to have relapsed into lethargy while waiting for more troops, led by Napoleon's brother Jerome, to move up to the front.[125] This was crucial in reducing the time that the Netherlanders were so exposed at Quatre Bras, enabling them to hold on.

However at 2 p.m., as the sun blazed down on the hottest day of the year, a cannonade finally announced the French main attack. Against it Perponcher's single division, according to Mike Robinson, whose mammoth work has brought the battle into focus at last, 'occupied a position that would not have been crowded if it had been held by four':[126] an extended line of the 5th Militia and the 27th Jäger under the command of Major General Willem Bijlandt. Twelve guns and four howitzers faced forty-two French cannon, Wellington was absent and his promised support was still several kilometres away.

Ney, mindful of Reille's warning, initially skirted the wood and launched an echelon attack north-eastwards against the farms to the south of the cross roads and the Netherlands line. Bijleveld's horse artillery slowed the advance by attacking the French right flank until a devastating counter attack blew up an ammunition wagon, disabled a howitzer and killed several horses, forcing him to save the battery by withdrawing out of range. The foot battery under Colonel Stevenart kept up a flanking fire against the French left until Ney turned a direct barrage on his position. Stevenart was killed, several of his officers wounded, and four of the eight guns were destroyed; the loss of the draft horses the day before, and the maiming now of more, meant that the remaining artillery pieces could barely be saved by the survivors – one limber was destroyed in an explosion,[127] and the men 'remplacent les chevaux manquant aux pieces par ceux des servants' (*replaced the lost horses with those of the support staff*)[128], almost certainly inferior and nervous animals. In addition, the under-trained gun-teams had halted too close to each other and there was no room for them to turn; attacked by waves of Red Lancers, the men were reduced to defending themselves with short swords and even the ramming staves.[129] There had been no troops available to protect the batteries, and still there was no allied cavalry on the field.

For the first two hours the Prince of Orange was in sole command of the dangerously extended line, and he acquitted himself well. The force and speed of the French attack left two Nassau battalions in an exposed position well to the southwest and parallel to the French advance. As the centre wavered, he quickly ordered them to thread their way north through the concealing woodland, thus shortening the defensive line and enabling them to reinforce the centre. He had stationed himself just behind Stevenart in a fully exposed position, and to safeguard the struggling battery, he calmly sent orders for his last reserve – the 7th Line battalion – to back him up. Then, according to a veteran, he encouraged the 5th militia and 27th Jäger to advance: '[Hij] stelt zich aan het hoofd van Westernberg's bataillon, en wekt door zijne toesprak den moed dier jonge soldaten.' ([He] *placed himself at the head of Westernberg's battalion and roused the courage of the young soldiers with a stirring speech.*)[130] The print shows the first French advance, as the Prince, with Westenberg on

EERSTE AANVAL DER FRANSCHEN, DOOR NEERLANDS ONSTERFELIJKE KRIJGSHELD, AFGESLAGEN
bij Les quatre Bras, den 16 Juny 1815

Fig. 4: Prince of Orange at Quatre Bras (Rijksmuseum, Amsterdam FMH6001-B)

the left, encourages his men forward past the wreckage of an artillery battery.

Only nineteen out of these four hundred and fifty recruits had ever seen action before. Nevertheless they pressed forward under the severest bombardment. Colonel Westenberg afterwards attributed their courage to the presence of the Prince, which may well have been a factor; but he himself had, in French service, been an officer of the Pupilles de la Garde Imperiale, so had experience of leading and inspiring young soldiers, which he was renowned for doing with intelligence and humour. In response to the cry of 'Lang Leve de Koning', they marched steadily on over their wounded and dying companions, and established a new forward line by the farm of Gemioncourt, well south of the crossroads. They deployed in the two-deep British line adopted in drills by the Prince, but without reinforcement this was pathetically inadequate. (The Nassauers, incidentally, still adhered to the continental tradition of a three-deep line.) They were exposed on two sides to hundreds of experienced French tirailleurs dodging through the tall rye as they aimed for the officers without whose support and encouragement the battalion wavered. A charge of French Lancers with their nine-foot spears followed; the sight terrified the young Dutch troops though despite their confusion they recalled enough drill to form a ragged square where they learnt, in Robinson's words, 'a valuable lesson about the impotence of cavalry against steady infantry'.[131] Robinson quotes a British sergeant's description of such an engagement as musket fire was opened from a square,

> Riders, cased in heavy armour fell, tumbling from their horses. The horses reared, plunged and fell on the dismounted riders. Steel helmets and cuirasses rung against unsheathed sabres, as they fell to the ground; shrieks and groans of men, the neighing of horses, and the discharge of musketry, rent the air, as men and horses mixed together in one heap of indiscriminate slaughter.[132]

The advance of dense columns of French infantry at last broke the Dutch and forced a retreat back to Quatre Bras itself as the Lancers speared them and rode them into the ground.

The arrival of Jerome with a further seven thousand eight hundred men (almost exactly the number of Netherlanders who had originally faced the French) enabled Ney to turn his attention to the Bois de Bossu. The Prince decided on desperate measures, and he called for volunteers for a counter-attack. Every man from the mauled remains of the 5th Militia stepped forward, and with the Prince riding at their head, they flung themselves once more from the centre against the enemy, still keeping the crossroads intact.[133]

Saxe-Weimar and his Nassauers were stationed in the Bois, providing the intermittent fire which had deceived Ney. This, of course, made his ammunition problem ever more acute, and he sent a messenger to the Prince asking for support. The man never returned. Saxe-Weimar recorded twenty-five years later: 'toen ik zag dat ik aan alle kanten omsingeld werd en mijn mannen gebrek kregen aan munitie, trok ik mij in goede orde terug.' (*When I saw that I was surrounded on all sides, and my men lacked ammunition, I pulled back in good order.*)[134]

They were not alone. The 7th Militia who had been ordered by the Prince to the extreme right of the line along the eastern edge of the wood, were in the greatest danger as Jerome advanced; one of them Corporal Pieter Wakker, recalled the order, unfamiliar to continental troops, to lie down supported by the elbows to aim their muskets, though he quickly realised its importance, the enemy 'dacht dat wij veel sterker waren dan dit inderdaad het geval was' (*thought that we were much stronger than was actually the case*)[135] 'achter ons was een digt bosch en voor ons een magtige vijand … wij verloren reeds duizend mannen.' (*Behind us was a thick wood, before us a mighty enemy … we had already lost over a thousand men.*) An exaggeration, but unsurprisingly they also retreated through the wood.

The Prince was aware that, despite being heavily outnumbered, he was still only facing part of the French army, and, concerned that the French might make a simultaneous thrust at Nivelles, he sent an order to Chassé and his third division to fortify the town. Since no British reinforcements at all had yet arrived, let alone the desperately needed cavalry, he had also ordered his own light cavalry to Quatre Bras. It is difficult to see how any commander could have done more than this "incompetent youth".

This cavalry finally began to arrive at around three thirty having struggled for nine hours along congested roads in the blazing sun. The men had halted behind the crossroads to feed and water the exhausted horses when the urgent order came to advance; as the squadrons scrambled to obey, an inexperienced colonel (recently returned to the colours after eighteen years in civilian life) panicked and ordered the charge before they were properly formed. As the ragged lines spurred forward through the rye, the hapless Colonel Boreel was riding blind. On bursting into the open, he saw the enemy squares well to his right, and his order to wheel caused even greater confusion. All cohesion was lost and they were overwhelmed by a disciplined counter-charge by the Lancers.[136]

The chaos coincided with the arrival at last of some of Wellington's reinforcements – British soldiers who were unlikely to forget what they saw. As Vels Heijn admits, Sir Thomas Picton's men of the 5th Division, marching up to the line convinced 'dat zij voor anderen de kastanjes uit het vuur moeten halen' (*that they alone must pull the chestnuts out of the fire for others*), arrived 'op een rampzalig ogenblik bij Quatre Bras'. (*at a disastrous moment at Quatre Bras.*)[137]

Even worse, there now occurred one of the cases of mistaken identity that would be a feature of the whole Campaign. Picton's Scots, seeing Van Merlen's cavalry dressed in blue or green, in full retreat, while their officers tried to rally them in their accustomed battlefield language, understandably assumed they were French and opened fire. As Elias van Balveren, a major in the 6th Dutch Hussars, laconically observed, 'a corps of Scottish troops, which was posted on the low ground ... received the enemy [sic] with arms at the ready.'[138] Since the British parade-ground instruction had been to aim for the horses, many of these went down, leaving their riders impotent because of the lack of reserve mounts.

The delay in reinforcements was entirely due to the confusion caused by the different sets of orders the Duke had issued on the evening of 15 June. Messengers riding through the unfamiliar terrain at night often failed to find their objective; it was difficult even to identify the wooded tracks, and commanders had barely received one set of orders before a countermand arrived. Messages were meant to be taken back by the same hand, inscribed with the time of receipt, but the Acting Quartermaster, Sir William de Lancey, received virtually no confirmation so he could not be sure of the whereabouts of any individual battalion or regiment. In addition, it is most unlikely that he even had enough messengers available to carry different orders to all units twice in four hours – many must have been given instructions to contact two or more; Mercer would seem to endorse this when he noted that he was woken in the early hours by his servant who handed him

> A note which an orderly hussar had left, and ridden off immediately … The note had nothing official in its appearance… and was totally deficient in date.

The information de Lancey passed to Wellington in the morning was far more optimistic than accurate.

The few roads suitable for the movement of troops had become congested. Rebècque himself had had to mediate between the divisions of Chassé and Lieutenant General Charles von Alten as they deadlocked in Nivelles. Alten pulled rank and forced his way through Chassé's men, though that meant that his troops had to press on through the stifling heat, while the Netherlanders were able to snatch some rest by the side of the road for an hour or two. Around Braine-le-Comte a Hanoverian cavalry brigade with accompanying baggage train, coming up from Mons, converged with British units hurrying from the west, and after some hours of jostling, eventually formed one great column of sixty thousand men marching along the single road to Quatre Bras.[139]

The road south from Brussels was more open, but there seemed to be little sense of urgency. For example, the bulk of Picton's division had set off from Brussels at five a.m. and was ordered to concentrate at Mont St. Jean. Here they stopped to cook breakfast some hours later. Wellington passed them with a friendly greeting on his way to Quatre Bras, but still appeared totally relaxed and did not amend the orders, despite having assured the Prince the night before that reinforcements were already on their way. It has been suggested that even at this late stage, he felt he might have to swing them to the right along the western road to block a flanking attack. Picton's men did not embark on the remaining fifteen kilometres of their march until after midday; Frederick Pattison of the 33rd recalled marching and singing towards the roar of artillery, and then halting again 'to devote a couple of hours to rest and refreshment'.[140]

Nevertheless, according to Sergeant Robertson of the Gordon Highlanders, 'we were all anxious to assist … eager to show one little isle of the sea that would brave [the enemy's] colossal strength and defy him to his teeth',[141] as they closed up behind the fragile Netherlands line against a column of advancing French. The arrival of the reinforcements meant that the Netherlanders could pull back at last. General Willem Bijlandt's brigade 'almost totally in ruins, having been heavily outnumbered from the start,'[142] headed for the comparative safety of the Bois de Bossu, through the British infantry who, again, would see only 'a headlong flight' or 'a cowardly retreat'. The Netherlanders had in fact, in Hofschröer's words "just managed to buy the time needed for reinforcements to arrive",[143] but misunderstanding and ignorance would now influence British memories.

As Wellington took over command on his return from his meeting with Blücher, and as Picton's men and Charles Alten's 3rd Division tipped the numerical balance through the afternoon, Ney was hard-pressed. Some Netherlanders and Nassauers remained in the field, taking part in isolated episodes of desperate fighting, but their main contribution was over as the British and Hanoverian reinforcements replaced them. As most of their battered battalions streamed back along the Nivelles road to their headquarters to regroup, the advancing troops from that direction, 'ignorant of their losses and oblivious to their ammunition shortages', spread the word that 'being disaffected to the cause [they] had left the field like traitors'.[144]

However, many of these troops soon realised on arrival at the crossroad the gravity of the situation. Sergeant Robertson, facing a massive column of French infantry, looked for supporting artillery: 'we had none up yet, none with which to oppose them'.[145] The complaint would be general among the veterans. Thomas Morris of the 73rd, witnessing the carnage, wrote: 'though it is treason to speak against the Duke … we had neither artillery nor cavalry in the field' – all he could see was 'a brigade of German artillery [actually the Netherlanders] and some few Brunswick horse'. He had heard that they were quartered too far away, but he poses a significant question, 'should it have been so?' – His own battalion had arrived after a thirty kilometre march in the blazing sun, and was ordered to advance through the seven-foot rye. Attacked by French cuirassiers, Morris had the honesty to record: 'we were compelled to retire, or rather to run to the wood.'[146]

Misunderstanding continued: a corporal of the 42nd Foot noticed a group of cavalry in the distance. A Peninsular veteran who had been held captive there by similarly uniformed men, he warned his commanding officer, but was assured that they were Oranien-Nassau troops, others identified them as Brunswickers. Either way, they were ordered to allow the horsemen to pass through their ranks,

> I think we stood with too much confidence, gazing towards them as if they were our friends, anticipating the gallant charge they would make on the flying foe.[147]

Suddenly these men launched into a gallop, and trampling down the British skirmishers, hurled themselves upon the hapless men as they scrambled from line to ragged square. Once more the description of the Allied Army as 'an ethnic and sartorial ragbag' was validated. Wellington himself had a narrow escape when he failed until too late to see that the fleeing Belgians were intermingled with their French pursuers; the latter caught sight of him and swung in his direction. At full gallop up the chaussée, he swerved towards a ditch concealing men of the 92nd, whose Colonel, with enormous presence of mind, ordered them to duck down; Wellington spurred Copenhagen into an enormous leap over them, and on a further command, they stumbled to their feet and their muskets brought down friend and foe alike among the pursuers.

Reinforcements were still arriving piecemeal. Private George Hemingway of the 33rd later wrote to his mother describing the march up to Quatre Bras, 'we met broken faces, legs and arms, and others lying dead on the ground …we got it pretty hot.' He was later stationed in the Bois de Bossu, 'we got out, but we mustered pretty small.'[148]

Wellington's orders on the evening of 15 June had only ordered Lord Uxbridge's cavalry to concentrate at Enghien (over forty kilometres from Quatre Bras). They would arrive, with Mercer's detachment of the Royal Horse Artillery, by forced march at nine o'clock that night as dusk fell and the battle was over. The Netherlanders, at desperate cost to themselves, provided the only cavalry or artillery on the field for almost the whole day.

The Brunswick contingent, the Black Legion, marched in late in the afternoon, and at first were positioned near Gemioncourt where they endured a fierce bombardment from Ney's twelve-pounders. The Duke calmly sat his horse, smoking a pipe, as one of his colonels fell dead and another had his left arm torn off by a shell splinter. Ordered forward he led his Uhlans against the first infantry wave of Jerome's Division, but they were driven back in confusion. Brunswick then placed himself at the head of his two battalions of infantry and advanced again; twenty-five yards ahead of them he was a clear target, and his horse went down. Staggering to his feet, he was hit by a musket ball which smashed his left hand, passed into his stomach and lodged in his liver. Still conscious, he was carried away, but before a surgeon could be found he was dead. As the news filtered through to his young soldiers, they wavered and lost heart. (It is an indication of the sorry relationship between the Prince Regent and his wife that Princess Charlotte had to wait for her father's permission before she was allowed to send condolences to her mother.)

Meanwhile battle still raged in the Bois de Bossu where Brunswickers, Netherlands militia and a few Nassauers hung on in the northern part while the French held most of it. The undergrowth was full of corpses and smoke swirled round the trees so that men on both sides were only reacting to vague silhouettes. Simultaneously two Regiments of Foot were ordered to march eastwards through the wood to gain the open ground and the Charleroi road South of Quatre Bras. "Friendly fire" must have been the result as the defenders became aware of figures approaching through the trees on their right flank, or even behind them. Some of them finally gave way and a "foreign" retreat was once more noted by the British. As the regiments left the wood and approached the crossroad, they found themselves back in the fields of rye; cut down and trampled, the crop reminding one veteran of the straw still thickly laid in London streets at times of sickness to muffle the rumbling traffic. In a terrible world they stumbled over dead and mutilated Highlanders who were 'most provokingly distributed' as one of them put it.

> The roaring of great guns and musketry, the bursting of shells and shouts of combatants …while the squares and lines, galloping horses, mounted and riderless, mingled crowds of wounded and fugitives (foreigners) [sic], volumes of smoke and flashing of fire struck out a scene which accorded admirably with the music.[149]

Wellington gradually regained tactical control, but only just, and it should be remembered that it still took the British reinforcements another five hours to dominate the field. Around six o'clock four exhausted battalions of Foot Guards arrived, having marched fully forty kilometres from their base near Enghien, and had immediately to be committed to battle. They were part of the Prince of Orange's Corps, and he ordered them to advance into and clear the Bois de Bossu. Many collapsed as they fought their way through the dense undergrowth, and were kicked and accused of cowardice by their sergeants following behind. The confusion was total, with no points of reference among the trees all sense of direction was lost, and isolated groups of French, British, Nassauers, Netherlanders and Brunswickers tackled any figure they saw in the woodland gloom – as Robinson writes, 'it was safer to shoot first and worry about consequences afterwards'. His impassioned description bears witness to the sacrifices of the entire Campaign; as hundreds of muskets spat smoke and fire through trees and undergrowth,

> Dozens of men dropped to the ground, limbs torn away, leaving stumps of shredded sinew and shattered bone. Balls smashed into torsos, creating sucking wounds of torn flesh, contaminated with leather and cloth. The brains of some men spattered across the faces of others, jaws were ripped away and horrified screams rang out as young men realised that the great gouts of blood pumping from severed arteries were their own, their young lives ebbing away into the mulch that would be their final resting place.[150]

The French brought artillery up to the edge of the wood and fired indiscriminately into it, but under that cover the French infantry finally streamed away, and the British commanders ordered their men out to regroup – "a muster very small".

The Prince of Orange still also commanded Alten's Division which was a key element in Wellington's defence, and as battle raged in the wood, he was central to a battlefield crisis for which he would afterwards be held culpable. A reconnaissance unit had penetrated well forward, west of Gemioncourt farm, and reported a large body of French cavalry forming into detachments there; when it returned to report, the commander sent an urgent message to the exposed 69th regiment to form square to receive cavalry. At the same time a messenger was sent to inform the Prince, but never reached him because his horse was shot and he was trapped under the carcass (a situation which would occur again and again at critical moments). Against the background of an artillery bombardment through which cavalry would not advance (but which Ney had ordered in order to soften up the opposition) and with his vision blocked by the tall standing rye, the Prince only saw one of his regiments forming a target square, and reasoning 'logically' as Hamilton Williams admits, ordered them back into line in order to support the advance Picton was in the process of making on Gemioncourt.[151] As the hapless men of the 69th tried to obey, they were overwhelmed by Kellerman's fabled cuirassiers. Kellerman, for the first time in his life, had queried an order, pointing out he had only a single brigade against a force of twenty-five thousand men and suggesting he should wait for reinforcements. Ney told him, 'Charge with what you have, the fate of France is in your hands ... take your cavalry and ride them down'.[152] French cavalry charges were usually launched at the trot (making them of course much easier to control than the wild 'hunting-field' gallops of the British) but on this occasion Kellerman led them at the gallop to conceal from his men how outnumbered they were. It was almost suicidal, but it succeeded in cutting the 69th to pieces and taking their colour.

Robinson asserts that 'even battalions with a far better view of the field were surprised by the rapid turn of events', since the cavalry had been in ambush behind the tall towers of the farm buildings and only the forward reconnaissance had been able to pick them out. It was certainly a command mistake by the Prince and one with grave consequences, but an understandable one, rather than the "reckless stupidity" for which some British writers have blamed him.

David Hamilton Williams, however, identifies, in this context, a certain Major Lindsay whose order to the 69th mistakenly left an open side to their square into which the cuirassiers could charge to create havoc. Since his source appears in the papers of William Siborne, whom he accuses of deliberate concealment of anything which might in the least way undermine the glorious British achievement, this might be true – the Prince becoming a convenient scapegoat to protect an Englishman's reputation. These papers reveal a letter from an eye-witness who recounts the Lindsay story, adding, 'Major Lindsay regretted the order till the day he died'.[153] – it remained in Siborne's file but he never used it.

Siborne served as an ensign during the occupation of Paris in 1815, and in the 1830s and 1840s (like Löben-Sels) he began to collect the memories of all surviving British officers, initially to build a topographical model of the battlefield, and later to form the basis of a two-volume history. His careful editing of the correspondence he received resulted in work (followed slavishly by all early English-speaking historians) which relied heavily on the conviction that the Netherlanders' contribution to the Campaign was, at best minimal, at worst disastrous. Their reputation could only begin to recover when further research about thirty years ago revealed Siborne's editorial technique. His anti-foreign prejudice can be summed up by a single editorial quote,

> The Dutch-Belgians commenced a hurried retreat, not partially and promiscuously, but collectively and simultaneously.

Wellington was to claim in his despatches that he had had 'a sufficient force to engage the left of the French army at Quatre Bras' (as opposed to the right wing under Grouchy which was engaging the Prussians at Ligny),[154] but as Charles Chesney points out, even by the end of the day,

> Wellington had at Quatre Bras three-eighths of his infantry, one-third of his guns and one-seventh of his cavalry. Truly in holding his own the great Englishman owed something that day to fortune.[155]

And, it should be added, to the Netherlanders. In reality it had been a day of short-term tactics on both sides; Wellington's cool head had triumphed over Ney's uncharacteristic performance.

The day's casualty figures were shocking, it was one of the very few of the Duke's battles when he had suffered more than the enemy. The American historian, Jac Weller blames these 'excessive losses' – which he estimates as four thousand five hundred, just over a quarter of them, Netherlanders – on the ineptitude of the Prince of Orange, the lack of effective cavalry and ground which the commander had not chosen – the latter two entirely Wellington's responsibility, and the first a serious error.[156] Many of the men, coming from the west, had endured a long march in the heat with no time for rest, food or even drink before they had to be flung into battle. The Netherlands and Nassau infantry lost eleven per cent of their total, their cavalry sixteen per cent, and it would certainly be noticed that the figures included nearly four hundred missing. This category will always cause hot debate in any conflict: many Dutch and Belgians would find it easy to slip quietly away; though, equally, if wounded they might find civilian refuge preferable to the struggling medical officers on the Brussels road. An 'ooggetuige' (*eye-witness*), contributing to an early collection of letters from Waterloo, and revealing that many wounded from there were only being carried into Brussels on the following Thursday, specifically records that these were British: 'Belgen an Nederlanders hunne uiterste pogingen aanwenden om hunne eigene woonplaatsen to bereiken.'(*Belgians and Dutch made the utmost effort to reach their own homes.*)[157]

This explanation could apply to both infantry and cavalry, but for the latter the loss of their horses meant they were perforce out of action through no fault of their own – without horses they could play no further part. Accounts of Waterloo often refer to a desperate call for new mounts since the casualty rate among horses was enormous. The British and German troops could usually obtain them but, as has been explained, a shortage of horses was always expected to cause problems for the Netherlands army.

False assumptions were already being made. Edward Costello of the Rifles wrote:

> About 3 o'clock in the afternoon we arrived at four roads; at the time there was a smart firing going on in our front; this, I believe, was caused by some Belgians playing at long shot with the enemy.

Such misunderstanding would colour all accounts of the battle. It had actually been an encounter characterised in Rory Muir's words by

> rapid improvisation in a fog of late, partial and inaccurate information.[158]

As for the Duke, he had,

> fought the most confused battle of his career, more or less by accident....It was the nearest [he] had come to suffering a major defeat, and he still had to face a better general than Ney commanding a much larger force.[159]

CHAPTER 12

Preparation

A S THE MEN of both armies tried to sleep that night surrounded by the dead and dying, none were under any illusion that they had won anything more than a temporary reprieve. Ensign Macready had fought his first battle at the age of seventeen, and learnt much,

> No one slept the worse [for their surroundings]. Military men know this, but it appears incredible to the uninitiated that a few hours of glory should give the heart such stoical insensibility.[160]

News filtered through of the Prussians' heavy losses at Ligny, and Blücher's withdrawal north towards Wavre, while French campfires were clearly visible south of the crossroads. Supplies of meat had reached Quatre Bras, but the cooking utensils had been left behind, and one group decided to use polished steel cuirasses as frying pans. The veteran recalling this managed to imply that these were littered over the field, though of course it had meant unbuckling them from French corpses. The scheme worked well, 'only we lost a little bit of gravy by the holes which our bullets had made in them'.[161]

There was no room to lie down and Corporal Wakker described leaning on his musket, over which 'ik hing een kapotjas van een doden franschman, en daar sta ik goed dacht ik.' (*I hung the greatcoat of a dead Frenchman, and I thought I stood well there.*) Wakker's often quaint constructions and old-fashioned spelling may indicate that he was a clerk before his recruitment into the unit which had been raised in Amsterdam. His reminiscences are especially interesting since they represent the views (and enthusiasms) of a minor player – similar to the 'very small soldier', quoted in Lord Chalfont's history of Waterloo who, when asked for his impression of the battle, replied,

> I'll be hanged if I know anything about the matter, for I was all day trodden in the mud, and ridden over by every scoundrel who had a horse.'

At daybreak the Prince himself came to them, bringing bread, meat and brandy. Wakker wrote: 'Altijd even friendelijk, hij zat even als wij op den kalen grond… dat doet een soldaat goed als hij ziet dat zijn overste gelijk op deelt het moelijkheid.' (*Friendly as always, he sat with us on the cold ground … it does a soldier good when he sees that his colonel shares the same hardship.*)[162] If an officer's command performance includes a rapport between the leader and the led, there is no doubt that the Prince should score well.

Gerard Rochell of the 19th Militia was especially lucky since he was bivouacked on the road from Quatre Bras to Nivelles, and early on the morning of 17 June was able to buy provisions from peasants toiling up through all the ruin of battle to market,

> I thus had a lovely breakfast of bread, butter, eggs and cherries … and as these were the first cherries we had seen, we enjoyed them very much.[163]

A British officer of the Rifles also struck lucky; rather surprisingly given permission by his colonel to plunder a farmhouse, the men used furniture to build an enormous fire and proceeded to slaughter the penned stock,

> We had as delicious a breakfast of beef, pork, veal, duck, chicken, potatoes and other delicacies as I ever made an attack upon.[164]

The scale of the defeat that Blücher had suffered at Ligny, which Wellington only realised on the morning of 17 June (again because the messenger from Gneisenau had been intercepted), meant that a swift withdrawal from Quatre Bras was necessary to maintain contact with the retreating Prussians. Most of the army took little over two hours to march north to Mont Saint Jean, ten kilometres south of the outskirts of Brussels, for the last hour in torrential rain (further indications both of the city's previous vulnerability to any advancing enemy force, and Wellington's good fortune that the weather protected him from a speedier French pursuit). He had ordered Uxbridge's cavalry to protect the withdrawal and when French Lancers almost caught up with them at Genappe, there followed an action described by the Life Guards as a glorious engagement and by the soberly observant assistant surgeon, John James, as a rout in which 'two elite British regiments [ran] away at full speed'. Mercer's artillery was involved, and he blamed Uxbridge (in his influential memoir published long after Uxbridge's death) for losing his head and issuing confused and dangerous orders.

When Rochell reached Nivelles he was ordered through it to take the north-east road to Mont Saint Jean, but he found the town still blocked by troops as cavalry and infantry jostled through the gates. He was surprised by

> The amount of baggage on the road, especially that belonging to the English [which was] remarkable, and this caused a great deal of confusion and delays, and was plundered by their own people. [sic]

The mauled 27th Jäger had also had to return to Nivelles the night before to reclaim fresh equipment and ammunition; they took with them many of their wounded, and on the way met the Allied artillery, arriving too late to take any part. Mercer's reminiscence did not spare them. Assuming that they were in retreat, he spoke of

> The numbers thus leaving the field appeared extraordinary. Many of the wounded had six, eight, ten and even more attendants... My countrymen will rejoice to learn that amongst this dastardly crew not a single Briton appeared.[165]

The night of 17 June found most of Wellington's army gathered at Mont Saint Jean. The rain which had begun in the afternoon continued with an intensity which surprised even the Peninsular veterans. It was the worst weather 'since the memory of man' and it resulted in that "Flanders mud", so familiar to soldiers since. Few fires could be lit in the torrential rain so that the hunks of beef and mutton could not be cooked. Many men lay in the open where at least, as one of them remembered, the mud was washed from his clothes every time he turned over. Artillerymen crawled under their supply wagons, while the cavalry tried to rest, leaning against their restless horses – a dragoon unit bivouacked in a hollow which became waterlogged, and by morning was knee-deep.

The French had endured an even worse march north and fewer supplies since the retiring Allied Army had left the road a sea of mud which was almost impassable. The horses drawing the supply wagons strained and slithered, while yielding priority to the artillery meant that many of them slid into the bordering ditches, often trapping men under them in several feet of water. Lieutenant Martin of the 45th de ligne bitterly described the generals, their staff and even their servants 'who hardly ever bivouacked because of the weather', and found shelter in the villages,

> while we were soaked to the bones, scattered to the four winds, manoeuvring in the mud up to our knees in order to be in a position to cover these "monsieurs".

The sodden ground forced Napoleon to delay his planned eight o'clock attack on 18 June until after eleven, giving more time for preparation (and apprehension). Edmund Wheatley, a thoughtful and sensitive officer of the King's German Legion wrote a detailed account of his feelings as the two armies watched and waited,

> It is an awful situation to be in, to stand with a sharp-edged instrument at one's side, waiting for the signal to drag it out ... to snap the thread of existence of those ... hundreds of young men like myself ... whose acquaintance would delight and conversation improve me, yet with all my soul I wished them dead as the earth they tramped on.[166]

On the opposite side Martin watched as Napoleon reviewed his troops, riding along the line to acknowledge the enthusiastic cries of "vive l'Empereur" as the men hoisted their helmets or shakos on their weapons, promising him a great victory, while, ominously,

> perhaps only a thousand paces away, one could distinctly see on the
> opposite ridge, the English drawn up in a long sombre line of red.[167]

Even at this moment some contrasted their commander's 'dull white face
and heavy gait' with the lithe and dynamic young General Bonaparte
of twenty years before. But he was supremely confident and had that
morning rebuked his generals,

> because you have all been defeated by Wellington you think he is
> a great general, but I tell you he is a bad general, and it will be as
> easy as having breakfast.

The last few days had been Napoleon's first experience of Wellington on
the field, and would have made this opinion more than simply a morale-
booster. He had crossed into Belgium prepared to meet two concentrated
forces – the British and the Prussians – and deal with them separately;
since the Duke had been caught off-guard at Quatre Bras there had been
no concentrated British force. In addition, Napoleon considered that
Mont Saint Jean was a dangerous defensive position, so near to Brussels
and with the Forest of Soignies at his back. The truth is that neither
commander was at his best as they prepared to face each other for the first
and only time, but Wellington recovered himself when it mattered – his
conduct during the battle was undoubtedly his finest hour.

Napoleon was confident that their crushing defeat at Ligny would
cause the Prussians to retreat east along the supply line towards their
base at Namur, and he had ordered Grouchy to pursue them, 'with your
sword against his back'; he thus kept his army divided, detaching thirty-
three thousand men from the main force, but calculating that since this
would certainly prevent his two opponents from uniting against him
the risk was justified. He was unaware of two factors. The first was that
the Prussians were retiring not along their supply-lines to Namur but
north to Wavre, thus keeping them within reach of the Allied Army.
Gneisenau had modified his hostile attitude towards Wellington, and
even in Blücher's absence – for a time he was missing, presumed dead
after Ligny – issued orders to that effect and the Duke could therefore
be confident that Prussian support would be forthcoming. The second
factor was that Grouchy had become disorientated first by contradictory

intelligence from his scouts (the men retreating east were actually large numbers of deserters and the badly wounded) and, secondly, by a sequence of badly drafted communications from Soult, which included the order,

> Direct your movements on Wavre in order to draw near to us, place yourself in touch with our operations and link up your communications with us, driving before you those portions of the Prussian army that have taken this direction, and may have stopped at Wavre, where you should arrive as soon as possible ... You will follow the enemy columns that may be to your right with a few light units, in order to observe their movements and bring in their stragglers.

It had been a feature of Napoleon's command performance through the years that his calculations on the field had sometimes been vague or contradictory as his brilliant brain considered every possible contingency. Marshal Berthier – acknowledged as almost the Emperor's second self – had been able to iron out inconsistencies and his drafting of the subsequent orders was always clear and unambiguous. In addition, he would send messages in triplicate to ensure receipt (some of Soult's single Orders during the Campaign were delayed for many hours because of the terrain or accident).

Not surprisingly, Grouchy could make little sense of this one; leading a mixed force for the first time, and one already depleted and exhausted after Ligny, he had lost contact with the main body of the Prussian army altogether as it turned west towards Mont Saint Jean. As he marched north on the afternoon of 18 June, his corps commander, General Gérard, tried to persuade him to wheel left towards the gunfire which was clearly audible, but Grouchy, newly created Marshal, was too fearful of deviating from an order which emphasised Wavre so strongly. Afterwards he would find himself the scapegoat for French defeat, and certainly his appearance on the field would have been decisive, but he should not bear all the blame.

Elizabeth Longford describes Waterloo as 'so ponderously classical' that it should be divided into five acts; this is a useful device for analysing an eight-hour battle of ever-shifting fortunes, and it will be followed here.

CHAPTER 13

Waterloo Acts I and II

THE MEN OF the Allied Army had had a troubled night since isolated French patrols caused continual alerts, as Napoleon, worried that Wellington might use the darkness to retreat still further, probed the defences. As an old man, Corporal Wakker remembered his Prince's speech on that morning – he told them,

> Jongelui, houdt moed, ik zal voor u zorgen. Napoleon heeft plan om heden avond te zes ure in Brussel te komen en aldaar tot twaalf ure te plunderen ...... maar wij hopen den dertigste dezer maand in Parijs een flesch wijn te drinken.
>
> (*Young ones, be brave, I will look after you. Napoleon plans to reach Brussels at six o'clock this evening and to plunder it until midnight ... but we hope on the thirtieth of this month to drink a bottle of wine in Paris.*)[168]

Jan van Wetering, as befitted a veteran, made his preparations carefully. After a night on guard duty, he checked his weapons, washed as well as he could and 'trok mijn beste kleding aan' (*put on my best clothes*).[169] He would end this day as the only surviving sergeant of the 4th Militia, and on 7 July would be camped in the Bois de Boulogne as a triumphant end to the military career which he so carefully recorded.

The protection which the Netherlanders had given him at Quatre Bras had enabled Wellington to choose the ground on which to make a stand, and his tactical brilliance had not deserted him. A ridge, facing south and stretching from north-east to south-west forward of the village of Mont St. Jean commanded 'the great road' to Brussels and the spreading landscape of woods and fields of rye to either side of it. His defensive battles had almost always centred on a ridge – artillery could be positioned on top of it, skirmishers could spread down the slope and the main army could be concealed behind it. Sir Thomas Picton (who would meet his death there) grumbled about it, but southern Belgium is hardly rich in ridges. Various strongpoints in the form of buildings dotted the approach – when these were garrisoned they could provide flanking fire against an advancing force. North of the village the great forest of Soignies extended almost to Brussels; if a retreat were necessary, infantry could move through it but pursuing cavalry and artillery could not. Along the top of the ridge a narrow road, cut into the ridge – the chemin d'Ohain – ran roughly east and west, at right angles to the Brussels road; bordered by hedges and stunted thorn bushes, it would prove a hazard or a protection to either side. The Allied front line extended along the ridge and behind it lay the rest of the army, its numbers concealed from the French, whose every attack would be launched 'up a slope' – as the day wore on, a slope littered with the corpses of those who had gone before.

Wellington's battle-line was, as Saul David has pointed out, strangely lopsided.[170] There was still an obsession with the right flank which was heavily defended with massive reserves, the centre was relatively strong, but his left was covered by just two infantry divisions – those of Picton and Perponcher – both depleted by their engagement at Quatre Bras. In addition, seventeen thousand men, including the I Netherlands Division, were left at Hal (less than fifteen kilometres to the west). It was now obvious to the Duke that he was facing a frontal not a flanking attack, while the massive French advance at Ligny must have precluded anything except a central assault. Even on the early morning of 18 June, those men at Hal could have been ordered to join the main army, and on open roads, however bad, they would have arrived well before the Prussians. Wellington knew that Blücher's help would be crucial, and he was obviously counting on it within a short time, having no idea that the Prussians were going to have to fight every inch of the way through flooded streams, narrow village streets and ignited powder wagons as well as against the French VI Corps, and would not arrive in any strength until early evening. His possibly apocryphal exclamation, late that afternoon, 'Give me Blücher or give me night' certainly illustrated his desperate need for extra troops.[171]

The Battle of Waterloo began about midday with a French attack on the Chateau de Hougoumont, a collection of stone buildings forward of the British right. Its southern side was protected by a small wood, and the Nassauers' success in the Bois de Bossu having been noted, three of their companies were stationed there. Private Johan Peter Leonhard recalled his first sight of the chateau,

> The doors were open, one could see the freshly broken loopholes in the wall. Ha, I thought to myself, here you'll settle in but leave nevermore. Good night world.[172]

He and his fellows fought from tree to tree, exacting fifteen hundred casualties from Napoleon's massed columns. After an hour they were finally driven back and took refuge in the buildings themselves garrisoned by the Coldstreams, and together they held Hougoumont throughout the day against a far greater force, and despite fire gutting their defensive positions. Eleven French battalions were launched through the wood in a desperate attempt to clear the buildings. When their general was killed, the charismatic young Marquis de Cubières assumed command; already wounded at Quatre Bras and with his arm in a sling, he was thrown from his horse, and according to an eyewitness 'the English officers ... threw themselves in front of their soldiers to prevent them from killing him', and dragged him into the chateau where the wounded of both armies were laid side by side. The defenders of Hougoumont seem to have shown considerable humanity: a private of the 3rd Foot, Matthew Clay, recalled that when a party of French stormed one of the gates, they were driven out leaving behind a small drummer boy who had lost his drum – Clay concealed him in one of the stables.

The heroic defence of Hougoumont diverted one and a half French divisions from the main front – infantry which would be desperately needed by Marshal Ney elsewhere. Andrew Field graphically describes the battle for Hougoumont as 'a meat-grinder', steadily absorbing more and more men through the day. It seems clear from all the French accounts that Napoleon originally intended this attack as a purely diversionary one, drawing allied troops to their right flank while he drove his main offensive through the centre to gain the Brussels road and separate Wellington from Blücher.

At about one thirty Napoleon initiated Longford's "Act II" when "la Grande Batterie" of between fifty and eighty-four guns (there is little agreement as to the number), which had been 'softening up' the thinly defended British left, ceased to allow d'Erlon's column of 18,000 infantry to attack. For much of the time their main target had been Willem Bijlandt's brigade of Perponcher's Division. Every panorama and diagram shows these men at least a hundred and fifty yards forward of the main line which consisted of the sunken Ohain road behind which Wellington concealed his main body of troops, and every historian has speculated as to the reason for their exposed position. According to Longford 'they stuck out like a sore thumb' as the men stood firm in front of the ridge, 'their elegant blue coats with orange facings' presenting an easy target for the French guns.[173]

The arguments about Bijlandt's position and performance form a microcosm which demonstrates the difficulty, if not impossibility, of wholly accurate descriptions of any battle. The man in question was forty-four. A cadet at the age of twelve he had moved from Dutch service to British, commanding an infantry regiment in the East Indies and a cavalry one in Ireland. He returned to civilian life in 1802 and was recalled by King Willem in 1814. His British service seems to undermine one explanation offered for his isolation – that he was following continental practice (as at Ligny by the Prussians) of surveying an enemy advance from a forward slope.[174] Other guesses as to the reason include Chandler's 'presumably accidental';[175] while Saul David's suggestion of their acting as a communication with the already garrisoned farmhouse of La Haie Sainte[176] is possible since that lay two or three hundred yards to the south west. Hamilton Williams' theory – that they had been placed there the previous day as one of the outpost guards to the then left flank of the army as it marched back from Quatre Bras and had been forgotten by the high command[177] – may indeed be valid, and it focusses attention on the performance of Sir William de Lancey.

In the history of Waterloo, de Lancey holds an almost saintly status due to the moving diary kept by his young wife who nursed him on the field until he died of his wounds;[178] but the truth may be slightly different. Wellington's 'old right arm' from the Peninsula, George Murray, was on his way back from Canada where he had been sent as governor-general; his replacement, Sir Hudson Lowe, having been dismissed as 'a damned old fool'[179] who couldn't read a map, de Lancey – a man the Duke once described as 'the idlest man I ever met' was appointed; his assessment is perhaps borne out by the fact that Magdalene de Lancey remembered that from 8 June, 'fortunately my husband had scarcely any business to do, and he only went to the office for about an hour every day.[180] De Lancey's title was Acting Quartermaster-General, i.e. without full authority, in the expectation that Murray would reach the army before any hostilities began.

De Lancey faced enormous problems – the fact that orders had to be filtered through different national chains of command was one of them, and another was his unfamiliarity with the Low Countries (having served in the East Indies and the Peninsula). He had arrived in Brussels barely a month before and had probably had little time to see for himself the roads and dirt tracks over which his messengers must ride. But the night before Quatre Bras had presented him with his greatest challenge as the Duke's different sets of orders were despatched over hundreds of square miles of countryside. As mentioned in the previous chapter, he could have had little idea then of the whereabouts of any contingent, and matters were unlikely to improve much even over the next two or three hectic days. One of his written orders to a Netherlands contingent on 16 June shows the stress he was under – untimed, covered with blots and almost illegible, it needed a repetition before it could be implemented the next day.[181] It would not be surprising if he overlooked a single brigade of one of the foreign divisions.

Therefore, the reason for Bijlandt's dangerous deployment could be the simplest – human error; nobody remembered he had been placed there and as command attention concentrated on Hougoumont to the right, and the expected Prussian arrival to the left, his position was only noticed by Perponcher when he arrived at Mont Saint Jean from Nivelles.

There is similar disagreement among historians (and veterans) about the performance of Bijlandt's already mangled brigade. Chalfont places them there throughout the bombardment – 'badly shaken they withstood its pounding' – but the advance of d'Erlon's columns broke them and 'they disrupted the ranks of Picton's three brigades in their flight'.[182] Holmes certainly implies that they were still in place for the French attack, '[the French] forced back the first line of defenders [i.e. Bijlandt], and the Netherlands units fought a good deal better here than anglophone historians often suggest'.[183] Chandler refers to 'Bijlandt's Belgians' [sic] who 'bolted to the rear' even during the bombardment.[184] Pawly has them 'to the bafflement of observers' exposed for a full hour to the might of eighty-four guns.[185] Longford describes them retiring in disorder, booed by the Cameron Highlanders as they passed.[186] James Shaw Kennedy refers to Bijlandt's brigade which 'retreated... and placed itself against orders on the reverse slope'[187] ; since this was the position of Wellington's main force, one can query what the "orders" were. One historian even asserts (without reference) that 'contrary to many accounts of the battle, Bijlandt's brigade ... had been withdrawn from the forward slope of the Mont St. Jean ridge before the barrage started up'. However all of these accounts assert that the Dutch-Belgians took no further part in the battle, Longford describing them as camping behind the lines 'quietly smoking, cooking and waiting for the result.'[188]

Barbero refers to Bijlandt's position as an unhappy one: inexperienced troops in a two-line formation, mostly militia, four of the battalions greatly below strength since Quatre Bras, and a fifth 'in name only, a handful of men gathered round a standard'.[189] He avoids the question as to 'exactly why these troops found themselves in front of the sunken lane', stating it as 'the topic of a discussion that has not yet ended', but he also keeps them there through most of the bombardment, and blames 'the Dutch generals' for only noticing their exposed position too late to withdraw them before d'Erlon's advance.[190]

French accounts make it clear that d'Erlon's first contact was with blue-coated troops as well as red, i.e. Dutch-Belgian, and these must have been Bijlandt's brigade. Hamilton Williams describes the 7th and 8th Militia as standing up to D'Erlon's skirmishers until the latter suddenly parted to reveal a French column levelling four hundred muskets at them at close range – both battalions were virtually destroyed. Once again, Picton's Scots, whose orders were to remain lying down, encountered fleeing Netherlanders actually stumbling over them, and they received them with predictable spleen. However, within a very short space of time thereafter, this massive French attack (twenty-eight battalions) drove back the 95th Rifles 'in great haste', the artillery units on the ridge retired 'with considerable bustle' and the Cameron Highlanders wavered and began to fracture.

Vels Heijn blames Wellington for using the brigade as 'als een levende golfbreker ... zo absurd dat zelfs Engelse auteurs hierover hun vertontwaardiging hebben uitgesproken' (*a living breakwater ... so absurd that English writers have themselves expressed outrage.*)[191] Van Zuijlen records, 'the entire 1st Brigade [Bijlandt] ... and the artillery of the right wing fell back in order not to hinder the English cannon placed behind them, and also so as not to be exposed and uncovered to the enemy fire'.[192] He then describes them as re-forming 'in the same battle order' as before, just north of the sunken road. Rebècque also speaks of re-forming Bijlandt's battalions and moving them forward again. One British source which described the brigade as giving way, adds 'but [it] rallied again in rear of the ridge where it remained for the rest of the day' as a reserve if needed;[193] others simply record 'a broken flight'.[194]

Bijlandt himself describes facing the Young Guard under d'Erlon as the attack began,

> At this time I personally received an order from the Prince of Orange to move forward and to attack with the bayonet without giving the enemy time to deploy. A Scottish brigade [Picton] which was placed in rear of my position followed the movement and arrived almost at the same time upon the enemy. The confusion was great, the melée horrific, and it was in this confusion that I received a bayonet thrust in my thigh ...[195]

Mark Adkin is firmly of the opinion that the Dutch-Belgians were withdrawn by Perponcher from their exposed position *before* D'Erlon's attack, thus contradicting some of the British descriptions, but there are enough British accounts making it clear that they remained well forward, withstanding at least some of the advance, and certainly the barrage, to make it a point at issue. Corporal Wakker recalled looking down at his boot which was filled with blood although he had felt no pain; withdrawing, he pulled some lint from his pack and staunched the wound before returning to take the place of his sergeant whose left hand had been shattered by a slanting hit.

After Bijlandt fell, Colonel de Jongh of the 8th Militia, also wounded, had himself tied to the saddle and led another advance against d'Erlon. As a result some time later he was trapped under the saddle when his horse was killed; saved by two troopers he was then shot in the head but still managed to retain command. Wupperman in recounting this, points out, 'hoe onjuist het verhaal is dat de brigade van Bijlandt na den eersten aanval voor goed het slagveld zou hebben verlaten' (*how unjust is the story that Bijlandt's brigade left the field for good after the first attack*).[196] These Dutch sources at last clarify Bijlandt's actions and achievement which in English studies have been misunderstood and consequently vilified. A lieutenant of the 92nd refers to the hedgerow 'abandoned by "les Braves-Belges" – a scornful term which often appeared in the accounts of veterans. They were replaced by the two British battalions who, in their turn, were driven back, but, we are assured, 'only a little'. A valid question might be – why were Bijlandt's Netherlanders and Picton's Scots, entangled at Quatre Bras and both badly mauled there, placed together in the centre of the front line?

Edmund Wheatley had a long career of war service behind him, but admitted he had never seen such carnage – the artillery batteries with their draft horses and ammunition wagons had offered a wide target to "la grande Batterie" and many of the latter received direct hits, the massive explosions blowing men and animals to pieces. Another was partially set on fire and the terrified horses drawing it bolted across the field until some dragoons managed to race alongside and stabbed the horses down.

As the fragile left of his line wavered, Wellington had no reserves in place, and only a charge by the Earl of Uxbridge's heavy cavalry averted disaster as he launched it at the approaching French who were already within pistol-shot range; it was magnificently timed, but, as Uxbridge himself later admitted, 'the pursuit continued without order and too far'; forty per cent of his strength was lost in what Longford terms 'the endemic fault of the British cavalry'. This cavalry had always been convinced, despite long evidence to the contrary – from Prince Rupert of the Rhine at Edgehill to the Peninsula – that success must come from sheer velocity, the power of a phalanx at full gallop. The exhilaration of such action, launched by men accustomed to the English hunting-field, usually meant that any kind of discipline was forgotten; for most of the Household Brigade this was their first action, and, apparently, their training had never consisted of any instruction to re-form after the initial charge. Ignoring the bugle-calls to return, the cavalry splintered into isolated groups which then overran the enemy line – Uxbridge, realising he should never have led the charge himself (a mistake later committed by Ney also) struggled back to try and organise the reserve, only to find that most of them, including the Scots Greys (who were to achieve glory through Lady Butler's painting) had decided "to join the party". One gourmet trooper of the Life Guards happily remembered,

> We galloped at them [the Cuirassiers] and fairly rode them down; when they were unhorsed, we cracked them like lobsters in their shells, and by the coming up of the cannon afterwards, thousands of them were squeezed as flat as pancakes.[197]

However, the separated groups were immediately threatened by French Lancers sweeping behind them and blocking their return to the ridge. According to a French veteran, the ground was strewn with 'red jackets and grey horses' as his brigade 'threw themselves on Ponsonby's dragoons, swept them aside with a smile, destroyed them, and then returned to their positions'. The disaster validated Wellington's distrust of a cavalry arm; he had too much experience of its lack of discipline. It should, however, be emphasised that Uxbridge's initial charge certainly prevented a French breakthrough on the weakened left of the Allied line. (The Lancers' power was noted by the British, who had not fielded them during the Napoleonic wars. Many of their men suffered ten or twelve lance-wounds, often sustained in the squares when lances could be wielded from a greater distance than sabres and beyond the reach of bayonets. From 1816 a number of light dragoon regiments were transformed into lancers.)

Now, once more, a Netherlands commander acted on his own initiative and prevented even greater slaughter though no English source acknowledges it. Baron de Ghigny, surveying the field with all the experience of his long Imperial service, swung in with his light cavalry to assist the disorganised British. Watching him were the brigades of Hussey

Vivian and John Vandeleur, both Peninsular veterans, who maintained 'a masterly inactivity', not daring to disobey Wellington's orders to stand fast. General Müffling, who was nearby, was bemused when they assured him that they fully realised the danger their compatriots were in but 'the Duke of Wellington is very strict in enforcing obedience to prescribed regulations on this point'.[198] De Ghigny led a charge over the almost impassable trampled ground, the lime soil drenched by rain being of the consistency of mortar while the battered stems of rye wrapped themselves around the horses' legs. Eventually Vandeleur, to his credit, could stand by no longer, and he joined Ghigny in dispersing the harrying French which allowed the remnant of Uxbridge's men to struggle back: the Scots Greys had lost sixteen out of their twenty-four officers,[199] and less than half the men returned from a total of four hundred. Even these survivors were now powerless; most of them had lost their horses (many of which now caused havoc as, often injured, they careered madly all over the field) and without them the cavalry was no longer a functioning unit; as Barbero points out, 'a cavalry regiment was a bit like a single-shot weapon, you could use it only once'.[200] So now it was a British regiment's turn 'to take no further part'; no blame has ever been attached to its withdrawal, though perhaps it should have been. De Ghigny's own losses were over thirty per cent.

Almost simultaneously elsewhere on the field another Dutch general with long French service – Baron Trip van Zoutelande – noticed three squadrons of cuirassiers advancing on a Hanoverian square. He sent a lieutenant to his commanding officer, Uxbridge, requesting orders, but since the messenger could not find him through the chaos, Trip acted on his own. As he described years later, he allowed the French to approach as close as he dared, 'en in het ogenblik voordelig oordeelende liet ik de charge blazen' (*and when I judged the moment right I sounded the charge*).[201] His regiment of carabiniers killed or took prisoner fifty or sixty sabres, and once more, was joined by two English cavalry regiments. They drove the cuirassiers down the ridge, and were disciplined enough to observe the bugle-calls and return up the hill to deploy again behind the infantry. The lieutenant wrote many years later, in a further indication of the supply problems suffered by the Netherlands contingent,

If the 1st Regiment had been equipped with more useful weapons it could have done more, but to charge the Cuirassiers without armour and with poor weaponry was not easy.[202]

Once more, a crucial Netherlands intervention has been, surprisingly, ignored by most accounts, despite the fact that Trip is the only Netherlander mentioned in Wellington's despatch. It seems likely that the Duke's position at that moment was near enough for him to appreciate the move.

Shortly afterwards another regiment 'retired': the Cumberland Hussars formed a unit of newly recruited Hanoverians, with powerful horses and the usual decorative uniforms but no experience and little enthusiasm. Summoned into the line, they found themselves under musket fire and, led by their colonel, wheeled and took flight. Uxbridge's A.D.C., Captain Seymour, 'the strongest man in the British Army' was sent after him,

> he told me he had no confidence in his men, that they were volunteers and the horses their own property. All this time the regiment continued moving to the rear in spite of my order. I laid hold of the bridle of the Colonel's horse and remarked what I thought of his conduct.

The Hussars headed back to Brussels where they spread panic and confusion by shouting that Napoleon was on their heels; those who saw the unfamiliar uniforms leaving the field, immediately assumed they must be Dutch-Belgian. Pattison's specific description of 'a Dutch-Belgian' contingent which 'left the field like traitors.... [in their] French gray uniform with silver facings and sabre tash [riding] strong horses with switch tails' has been, until recently, accepted as further proof of Netherlands cowardice; however, from the detail given, it is surely a description of the Cumberland Hussars.[203] Creevey identified them immediately as he watched them galloping through the streets, and another observer wrote that they were accompanied by their women who were

> well mounted, riding astride on men's saddles ... with boots and trousers like dragoons, and wore a gown over all, with small round bonnets on their heads.

This unit was the only regiment (apart from the group of British sappers who withdrew precipitately along the Brussels road they were ordered to clear) who did not receive the Waterloo grant in 1817.

Perponcher had decided that of his two brigades, Bijlandt's depleted force was in the most need of his presence, and the other one, under Saxe-Weimar, was acting independently far to the left by some scattered settlements to the east of the main road, where it was expected that they would at an early stage make contact with the advancing Prussians. Once again, as at Quatre Bras, Saxe-Weimar was in the crucial position which protected the fault-line between the two armies, and with the 1st Battalion of the Nassauers at Hougoumont, he was left with two battalions and only three guns. The settlements provided an ideal defensive position since they were situated in a marshy area cut through with sunken lanes bordered by hedges, and Saxe-Weimar exploited it well. Behind him were some Hanoverian infantry and English cavalry, and he observes drily that the latter 'emerged on several occasions to execute charges although these mostly failed'.[204] Artillery fire caused many casualties, and fighting was fierce against an entire French division with the Nassauers experiencing their usual ammunition problems. The 2nd Battalion Oranien-Nassau (the personal troops of King Willem) had arrived from Germany only a few days before and had been given French muskets with no ammunition. Saxe Weimar wrote later: 'I was unable to secure English muskets for them – the whole of my infantry was armed with English muskets at this time.'[205] Confusingly, both Hofschröer and Barbero transpose this description, stating that Saxe Weimar's 2nd Nassau regiment was armed with French weapons and the Oranien-Nassau battalion with English. It is unlikely that Saxe Weimar's memory was at fault – he struggled with weaponry problems throughout the campaign – and, either way, the story of a fourteen-year old drummer boy who scrambled backwards and forwards through the firing line to fill his haversack with cartridges from the Hanoverian reserve, is worth recalling.[206]

CHAPTER 14

Waterloo Acts III and IV

A CT III FOCUSSES on the struggle for La Haie Sainte, the farmhouse situated three or four hundred metres in front of Wellington's centre, which had been an obvious target for both sides from the start. It could act as an obstacle to any French attack on the centre, but in enemy hands it would be "a dagger to the heart of Wellington's line". Garrisoned by men of the King's German Legion under the command of a British major, George Baring, its buildings were set within an orchard and formed three sides of a square, with a high wall bordering the Brussels road on the fourth side. The two entrances had previously been secured by heavy wooden gates, but in the wretched weather of the night before these had been burned as firewood, although the men must have known that it had to be defended the next day. Wellington reinforced them during the afternoon with three companies of the 1st Battalion of the Nassauers whom he detached from Hougoumont. Hamilton Williams gives these men the credit for creating a firing platform on the slanting roof, well above the vulnerable loopholes level with the road outside where the French had been able actually to grab the rifle-barrels of the defenders.[207] Also, the Nassau equipment included large field kettles for cooking, and these proved invaluable water carriers when the French set fire to the perimeter. There was plenty of water available, but Major Baring issued ever more despairing pleas through the afternoon as his ammunition supplies dwindled.

As Ney launched at least three vain attacks on La Haie Sainte through the afternoon, only succeeding in capturing the orchard while Baring's men retreated into the farmhouse itself, Napoleon became aware of troops approaching from the east, and when he realised they were Prussian (IV Corps under General Friedrich von Bülow) rather than Grouchy's force, he switched seven thousand men under Count Georges Lobau, originally deployed to support an attack on Wellington's left-centre, to the right to block Bülow's advance on the village of Plancenoit. Blücher, having promised Wellington at least one Corps, was responding with his whole force. General Johann von Thielman blocked Grouchy to the north in the under-acknowledged Battle of Wavre, while von Bülow was directed onto the French right flank, well south of the Allied line, where it was later joined by II Corps under General George von Pirch. I Corps under von Ziethen would be the last to arrive on the field since its route through the narrow muddy tracks from Ohain was the most difficult of all – these Prussians were the only ones that Wellington was able to detect from his central position, and their agonisingly slow progress added to the strain he was under through the day.

Napoleon, too, was under immense pressure. For two crucial hours in the late afternoon his attention was directed not so much to the Allied centre but to the threat to his right flank as Plancenoit changed hands again and again in fierce fighting; a French artillery officer defined the problem,

> Nothing is more likely to spread discouragement in an army, however brave it is, than to suddenly find itself attacked on its flanks and threatened with being turned, whilst it is vigorously engaged to its front.[208]

Lobau's force had been depleted by the transfer of one of his divisions to Grouchy, and it proved inadequate for the task. As it was driven back Napoleon was forced to send eight battalions of his reserve – the Young Guard – to its assistance. Many of the Young Guard were volunteers whose high morale compensated for their lack of experience, and, commanded by experienced officers, they managed to retake the village and hold it through three determined Prussian assaults. But finally they, too, gave way, and with time of the essence Napoleon threw in two battalions of his Old Guard with orders that they should attack with the bayonet.

In a duplication of the Hougoumont action more and more men were being drawn in to protect that right flank, and although they did actually stabilise the situation, those men would almost certainly have been able to pierce the wavering Allied line: all they could manage at Plancenoit was to delay the Prussians for a couple of hours though that was almost enough. Wellington's iron reserve was certainly tested to its limit during those hours – having expected the Prussians to support him by mid-morning, he had no way of knowing that their foremost advance was fully a mile south of his left, and he was reputedly praying for nightfall to rescue his dwindling force of as few as thirty thousand.

Baring's heroic defence of La Haie Sainte continued, and Ney, to whom for the first time Napoleon had delegated full command, was seemingly at a loss. He finally decided that he should encircle it by a frontal attack on the infantry battalions deployed behind the farm on a slight ridge and in a small sand-quarry. He was badly in need of the troops still tied down at Hougoumont or diverted to Plancenoit, but decided to launch a cavalry advance alone. It was tactical misjudgement on a grand scale, and his frantic conduct thereafter has led to speculation that he had either lost his head or – possibly – mistaken an infantry re-alignment to shelter from French artillery as a full-scale retreat. It would seem, however, that he initially ordered only a single brigade of cuirassiers into action, and that a massed charge was not his intention. Some have speculated that the rest of his cavalry spontaneously joined in (as the Scots Greys had done when Uxbridge charged), but this was most unlikely without a direct order from the Emperor, and it seems more probable that he did indeed order the full charge. It was a gamble but that would be entirely characteristic of Napoleon if, as Clayton believes, he calculated that the emergency on the right flank called for dramatic action in the centre. Because of the narrow front between La Haie Sainte and Hougoumont, Ney's five thousand cavalry actually extended far out to the left to threaten the whole of the Allied line (though leaving no room for manoeuvre). But the 'moving glittering mass' seemed, to the astonished men awaiting it, like a wave of the sea rolling inexorably to break over them. Thirty-six British and Hanoverian battalions and three Dutch and Belgian ones moved at once from line or column into square (movements which had already churned the agricultural fields into a sea of mud).

Parade ground discipline triumphed and not one square broke despite the alternating artillery bombardment and what an Ensign of the Foot Guards described as 'the awful grandeur' of the charge. 'One might suppose', he wrote, 'that nothing could have resisted the shock of this … they were the famous cuirassiers, almost all old soldiers, who had distinguished themselves on most of the battlefields of Europe.'[209] But this was the end for them – the mass was impotent; 'infantry was (and is) the only force with which ground could (and can) be held',[210] and the famed British infantry held firm. Donald Mackenzie of the 42nd Foot found time to admire 'such impetuosity as we had never experienced in the Peninsula since the French soldiers were fighting under the eye of their Emperor'. At one point, unable to get into a square, Mackenzie dropped to the ground and played dead as squadrons of cavalry thundered over him,

> I got a sword thrust as a sort of query whether I was as dead as I looked. However I lay motionless and the bullets whizzing about did not allow my inquisitive friend to prolong his enquiries.

Through the late afternoon the desperate Ney launched ever more cavalry attacks, many of which he led personally, interspersed with raking cannonades from two hundred guns; it was, as Vels Heijn marvels, 'complet waanzin wat hier gebeurt, heröische waanzin', (*what was happening here was complete nonsense, heroic nonsense*).[211] Both Wellington and Napoleon would have agreed. The squares held as officers threw the dead outside, dragged back the wounded and thrust new men in their place; allied casualties were appalling but the finest cavalry in Europe literally broke itself to pieces; the aim of one of their confused supporting artillery reserves was so bad that it wiped out a complete troop of its own men. Cavalié Mercer watched as the British case-shot caused utter carnage: the flanking troops were able to wheel away, but as the middle mass tried to turn back on itself there was chaos, men using the pommels of their swords to force their way through.

Just one of the Netherlands squares wavered under considerable losses – from lances and horse-pistols as well as the cannon – but a Hanoverian officer nearby noticed, 'the efforts of their gallant officers who gave their subordinates an excellent example [and] succeeded in bringing the men to a halt and leading them back to their former places'.[212] These officers included Perponcher who had already had two horses shot under him, and Rebècque himself whose journal relates how

> one of the battalions was put into complete disorder when a shell exploded amidst their ranks, I rode ahead of them and fortunately managed to bring them back.[213]

Captain Gronow of the 1st Foot graphically described his own square as 'a perfect hospital, being full of dead, dying and mutilated men'. He, at least, was an experienced soldier; for so many men of all nationalities, this was their first battle and one for which they had had little preparation. Sergeant van Wetering was also in square trying to control inexperienced men; standing just behind his captain, he moved forward as the latter collapsed, and simultaneously on his left a single bullet passed through two men killing them both, 'men zag niets dan gekwetsen van daar ons toekomen, de gehele linie was in kruitdamp gehuld.' (*We could barely see the wounded around us, the whole line was shrouded in gunpowder smoke*). A short time later the captain returned to the square since it was only the force of the explosion which had knocked him off his feet and stunned him for a while (a frequent occurrence though one which was the cause of de Lancey's death). He brought a message for 'Corporal Gerritson' – his wife had given birth to a son on the field and van Wetering was despatched to reunite them.

Wellington rode up and down behind the squares, his calm presence encouraging and heartening the desperate men. The print shows the battlefield in late afternoon. On the left the Prussians are, at last, in sight, and on the right a group of French prisoners are escorted by two mounted troopers. The Duke gestures in the centre, possibly to Uxbridge, while casualties from the cavalry attacks litter the whole area between the two armies. In the foreground three artillery batteries have been destroyed; on the right an exhausted man straddles a corpse. Wounded men are assisted by women – the one on the left may be one of those who distributed alcohol since a mule with panniers stands close by.

Although the British line was still intact, it had been terribly battered, and the Duke had used almost all his reserves. Colin Halkett, having

Fig. 5: The Duke of Wellington at Waterloo (Royal Archive, The Hague PR/2194) Jean Baptiste Madou. See also Plate 7

watched up to seven of his men felled by a single barrage 'as the clouds of cavalry waited like birds of prey' and seeing the rest 'sinking to the very earth with fatigue', sent a despairing plea to Wellington for help. He received the reply: 'tell him that what he asks is impossible, he and I and every Englishman [sic] on the field must die on the spot we now occupy.'[214] Napoleon, convinced that the English centre could not hold, now ordered Ney to take La Haie Sainte itself as a preliminary to driving through the English line, and after a pause, during which the dense smoke cleared revealing the full extent of the losses on both sides (and a British officer actually wondered if this might be the first battle in which there were no survivors),[215] "Act IV" began.

Through the day Major Baring had sent three ever more urgent messages requesting extra ammunition, and at the time of final crisis his men were down to four or five rounds each; Longford terms the lack of response 'one of the unsolved puzzles of Waterloo'.[216] The Germans used

Baker rifles of a smaller calibre than the ordinary muskets carried by the Nassauers at La Haie Sainte (who still had plenty of ammunition). There were problems over supply of the rifle ammunition elsewhere in the field (which may focus attention again on the hapless de Lancey) and as Ney himself led a combined force of cavalry, artillery and, at last, the rallied remains of some infantry summoned from reserve, the defenders had to resort to their bayonets before Baring ordered the retreat. A cultured and sensitive man, he felt the failure deeply.

> Never had I felt myself so elevated; but never also placed in so difficult a position where honour contended with a feeling for the safety of the men who had given me such unbounded proof of their confidence.

Less than half of the four hundred defenders managed to escape – some of them must have been Nassauers, and Barbero remarks that 'Major Baring preferred, in his account, not to elaborate on their performance, but they were inexperienced recruits …'[217] His inference is clear, but as explained, the Nassauers were far from inexperienced; they had already proved it at Quatre Bras and Hougoumont, and there could have been no hiding place at La Haie Sainte; however, yet again the easy option of assuming Netherlands' incompetence is taken.

Now the Prince of Orange, stationed on the plateau of Mont Saint Jean, made his second miscalculation. Charles Alten, commanding the 3rd Division of the Prince's I Corps, realised that Wellington's centre was at Ney's mercy and felt that the honour of his King's German Legion was at stake after Baring's retreat from La Haie Sainte. It may also be significant that Baring had served as Alten's A.D.C. in the Peninsula where Alten had served with the reputation of keeping a good table, but 'without being overly gifted',[218] although, against this, is the fact that he was the only foreigner whom Wellington allowed to command British troops there. He now ordered Colonel Christian von Ompteda at the head of the 5th KGL to retake the farm. Ompteda protested that such an attack would be suicidal in the face of such a massive force when two previous attempts had failed. But Alten repeated the order and appealed to the Prince for confirmation. As the overall commander Willem had to make a split-second decision and backed his immediate subordinate Alten.[219]

The 5th King's German Legion advanced and were taken on the flank by French cuirassiers who cut them to pieces before they could even fire their muskets. The remnants of the battalion (now numbering less than twenty men) attempted to regroup, and a young British officer saw 'Colonel Ompteda on his back, his head stretched back with his mouth open, and a hole in his throat'. The colour was taken and the Prince received the blame for a 'fatal self-sufficiency of military ignorance'.

Once again, it was a mistake, but the significance of La Haie Sainte in French hands could not have been lost on him; as the British staff captain, James Shaw Kennedy, explained in his memoir, it was very dangerous: 'it uncovered the very centre of the Anglo-Allied army, and established the enemy within sixty yards of the centre'. Furthermore, that centre was severely battered: Sir Peregrine Maitland's brigade of guards had been reduced to the strength of a single battalion, the allied cavalry present had almost lost its capacity for action and certainly its morale, and many companies were being commanded by sergeants, such was the toll on senior officers.

The buildings of La Haie Sainte now afforded protection, both to 'vast swarms' of tirailleurs who darted in and out pouring 'a most destructive fire on the constantly diminishing line of the allies',[220] and to Ney himself as he advanced up the main road on a broad front. His heavy cavalry forced the defenders into squares, which were then battered by the artillery he was able to conceal in the farm buildings so near to Wellington's line. But the broad front meant that Ney had no further reserves to make a final assault on the centre; he sent a desperate appeal to Napoleon for more troops, and received the reply, 'Where am I to get them, does he expect me to make them?'

It is just possible that Napoleon might, at that moment, have been able to stage a tactical withdrawal, retire to the border with a viable army and maintain his position, but such action was against his every instinct. He still held a reserve of fourteen battalions (out of his original thirty-seven) – Old Guard and Middle Guard – 'the Immortals' whom he always used to deliver the final blow, and whose reputation was feared by every British veteran. Ordering them forward he accompanied them as far as La Haie Sainte, but then turned aside with some of his generals, and handed them over to the already exhausted Ney: whether this was his own choice or in response to persuasion by his staff is uncertain. His brother, Jerome, fully aware of the crisis, was horrified, 'can it be possible that he will not seek death here. He will never find a more glorious grave'. The joy of his men when he seemed to be leading it into battle changed to disappointment, but he was about to commit a further act of betrayal. He sent officers to spread the word that the approaching troops were actually Grouchy's, come to fall on the Allied left flank while the Guard attacked the centre. Clayton tends to give Napoleon the benefit of the doubt, pointing out that the firing of von Ziethen's I Corps as it approached the left of Wellington's line, attacking the Nassauers under the impression they were flanking French, could have been Grouchy. He had, after all, (as he thought) ordered Grouchy to the field. But even if this was so, he was well aware that the most immediate threat to his men came from the powerful Prussian forces he was attempting to block. The French accounts do seem quite firmly to refer to a deception. Ney himself doubted later 'whether the Emperor was deceived', recalling his astonishment and indignation, while one of Soult's aides-de-camp went further – it was 'a significant lie'. This man had just returned from a reconnaissance to the right wing where he had witnessed the true state of affairs, 'I heard Napoleon give [that] order [about Grouchy]… and I cannot find words to describe the feelings I then suffered.'[221]

Wellington's dilemma was such that he had to turn now to the Dutch-Belgians. Probably, with some trepidation, he sent orders to David Chassé, four kilometres to the west, to bring up his brigade of the 3rd Netherlands Division into the line. Unengaged so far in either battle, they enthusiastically hastened to obey, but as they marched they came under heavy fire from the French batteries around Hougoumont. Once clear of these, there was a new danger – seeing blue-coated ranks advancing from the right 'uttering loud and repeated shouts (not English hurrahs)', the British artillery assumed a French flanking attack; with Mercer's guns trained on them, only the alertness of his colonel saved the advancing Netherlanders from annihilation.

The Allied line was faltering. Van Merlen's brigade had fallen apart when he was killed (in a charge on his old regiment, the Lancers of the Imperial Guard);[222] his Belgians refused to follow a Dutch commander and joined Ghigny instead; while another Netherlands regiment refused to obey an English officer, and was fired at by one of the infantry squares as they retreated. Howarth, following one of Siborne's more extreme descriptions, relates this incident to 'an excessively dissatisfied' Uxbridge, maintaining that 'there were still large numbers of foreign cavalry who had not been in action yet' and that the Prince had that morning asked the Duke to put all the Dutch cavalry under Uxbridge's command. Both these assertions can be contradicted by other accounts, but Howarth does touch on the important point that the rank and file probably did not know who Uxbridge was, and were reluctant to follow 'an excited Englishman who gave his orders in a language they could hardly understand and galloped madly at a force of several thousand French'.[223] These incidents illustrate the difficulty faced by a 'polyglot army' as the casualty list mounted. Major von Busgen, of the 2nd Nassau light infantry moving from Hougoumont to La Haie Sainte, later asserted that at no time 'was any commander under whose orders I was placed, named to me'.[224]

A regiment of Brunswickers – 'perfect children', according to Cavalié Mercer – whom Wellington had hurriedly switched to the centre, began to fall back, still stricken by the loss of their Duke at Quatre Bras. Colin Halkett had almost no men left to command when he was shot in the face, and those remaining fled. Some regimental colours were being sent to the rear (a sure sign of impending collapse) and most of the Duke's personal staff had been either killed or wounded. Ensign Macready remembered that 'fifty cuirassiers would have annihilated our brigade', as he waited for them to attack through the swirling smoke.

The reason they did not was that the Prince of Orange, realising he was the only commander in the whole sector left in the saddle, actually led a battalion of Nassauers commanded by August von Kruse in a bayonet charge on two Imperial Guard squares. There could be no supporting fire since all the artillery batteries in the sector were either destroyed or out of ammunition. Von Kruse wrote later that the Prince 'showed as much courage as foresight, despite having been in command on the plateau throughout the whole battle', and Barbero gives him the credit for the fact that, taken on the flank, the enemy wavered, giving time for British officers to reform some sort of ragged line against the renewed advance.[225] In a wild firefight, the Prince himself received a bullet in the shoulder and was rescued by his staff; as they lifted him down, his horse

Fig. 6: Wounding of the Prince of Orange (Rijksmuseum, Amsterdam FMH6017-B)

was killed outright. The print shows the moment of his wounding as he drops the left rein: troops on the left use their musket butts against a cuirassier since they, too, were out of ammunition. There is some artistic licence here with opposing infantry seemingly only a few feet apart and using muskets rather than bayonets.

He was carried – on a door – to the inn which served as an officers' hospital, where he waited his turn, and watched as his fellow aide-de-camp from the Peninsula – Fitzroy Somerset – endured the amputation of his arm. The Duke's own coach was then commandeered to take him and the Prince back to Brussels, from where Willem wrote proudly to his parents,

> Victoire, victoire. We have had a magnificent affair against Napoleon today ... it was my corps which principally gave battle ... I am wounded by a ball in the left shoulder but only slightly. A vie et à mort, tout à vous, Guillaume.

His boast was pardonably exaggerated but not unreasonable – all four divisions of his Corps had been in action, as against two of II Corps.

CHAPTER 15

Waterloo, Act V

THE IMPERIAL GUARDS advanced, driven on by their relentless drummers, the tall bearskins with red plumes making them appear as giants, and with the hurriedly regrouped British line barely holding, Edward Cotton, a sergeant major of the 7th Hussars who later acted as a guide to the battlefield, saw that 'the fate of the battle seemed to quiver on the beam'. One of the regimental surgeons remembered,

> it seemed as if the French were getting the best of it slowly but surely … a goodly number of experienced officers thought the same.[226]

Chassé, himself, wrote that when he arrived on the plateau of Mont St. Jean, 'there were no troops, not a single man belonging to the Allied Army between my division and the Garde Impériale'.[227] An English artillery battery to his left suddenly ceased firing, and he rode over to instruct them to continue only to be told that they were out of ammunition. Chassé's account is confirmed by Clayton's description of the Garde's advance,

> The allied artillery was remarkable for its silence. The Guard passed over the crest of the ridge and to their astonishment found the plateaus empty, except for the corpses with which it was littered.

Yet again a Netherlands commander used his initiative. Chassé explained to Baron Charles Nepveu, Rebècque's staff officer,

> the reasons which caused me to advance without having received any orders… I saw the Garde Impériale advancing while the English

troops were leaving the plateau *en masse* and moving in the direction of Waterloo; the battle seemed lost....

He ordered his divisional artillery forward to focus on the French advance, and then placed himself at the head of his brigade of line, militia and jäger battalions, and drawing his sabre told them – according to a letter Lieutenant Hendrik Holle wrote to his sister – 'keep calm, depend upon my command and especially upon your brave officers, the battle is not yet decided, but how great it will be for you to have taken part'.[228] According to his admiring aide-de-camp, Frederik van Omphal, the General 'manoeuvred in such a way that the head of his column was opposite to the one attacking when a height was reached, which had hidden our troops until this moment'.[229] With the cry of 'Oranje boven, lang leve onze Koning' the brigade pounded down the slope against the French advance. Ensign Macready wrote in his journal that they were 'drumming and shouting like mad with their shakos on top of their bayonets' and as he watched them sweep over the piled corpses of so many of his comrades, his utter relief led him 'to laugh with them'.

Macready's recognition of the debt he owed them was not matched by Wellington's. Chassé was to receive no acknowledgement from him after the battle, and that disregard is important. Mark Adkin in his invaluable work realises that the reference in Wellington's first Dispatch to the Belgian 'General Vanhope' at the head of a brigade of infantry, is wrong – no such officer existed – but he corrects this by interpreting it as 'Detmers'. Hendrik Detmers did indeed command 'a brigade of infantry', but he was a colonel under the overall command of Chassé, not a general, and his own report[230] does not mention his commander, concentrating instead on his own part in the final advance. Detmers records that the three battalions under his command joined the line,

> His Excellency the commanding general [Wellington] then placed himself at the head of the entire brigade ... and thereupon pursued the enemy in a lively manner with the entire line, until Major-General Constant de Rebècque brought us the order to halt.

Wellington and Rebècque were certainly together at the head of their men in this deciding charge. However, Chassé's description of his arrival on the field arguably indicates that his action *precedes* that final charge, and Macready clearly asserts that he and his companions were saved 'by a heavy column of Dutch infantry', not a coordinated charge. Huw Davies describes the incident, though again without mentioning Chassé personally,

> Part of [the Garde] was engaged and repulsed by tenacious Dutch and Belgian troops who successfully charged [them] whilst the 33rd [Macready's] and the 69th Regiments briefly wobbled.

and he, too, separates this from the general advance *ordered* by Wellington – Chassé makes clear that he was acting 'without orders'.[231] Chassé, himself, reports that

> At the moment I forced the French to yield I had the Allied cavalry next to me advance so as to support my attack, this movement was followed shortly thereafter [sic] by the entire infantry and cavalry, against which the enemy soon retreated in complete disorder.

These Dutch accounts, published by John Franklin, would certainly seem to indicate that Wellington's (justified) initial distrust of Chassé led him to ignore the General's achievement, commending instead the later action of one of his subordinates whose name was anyway misrepresented. It is clear that the Dispatch was written by an utterly exhausted man, possibly even, as some have suggested, almost in a trance. As he told a friend,

> While in the thick of it I am too occupied to think of anything; but it is wretched just after…. Both mind and feelings are exhausted.

So the bleak and reticent tone of the Dispatch can be excused – but in holding himself aloof for the next thirty-five years from all comment and discussion, this was one of the grave injustices to thrive.

In a letter to the Prince, Chassé also mentions seeing far to his left as the Guard wavered 'the enemy moving on a small height'; galloping over he found a Captain de Haan and a few soldiers of the 19th Militia whom he ordered into a flank attack (similar to the much praised one which Sir John Colborne was to launch on the right though, needless to say, it is not mentioned in English studies):

> [De Haan] jumped over the hedge, reformed the line of about fifty
> men and the murderous fire he inflicted caused death and confusion
> among the enemy's lines. He took advantage of their confusion and
> advanced with the bayonet against them. I had the unspeakable joy
> to witness 300 Cuirassiers run away from 50 Dutchmen.[232]

Colborne and de Haan formed part of Wellington's glorious final charge
which he timed to perfection. He waited in silence, fully exposed on
the ridge, until the enemy was barely sixty yards away; behind him,
concealed from the advancing French were fifteen hundred Guards led
by Maitland – the remnant of his command after their mauling in the
Bois de Bossu. A few remaining batteries of artillery rained canister on
the French. An observer spoke of 'long lanes of light' through the dark
mass, as entire ranks of men were felled by a single ball. Three quarters
of the way up the ridge the French seemed to pause and resorted to
muskets rather than bayonets.

The Duke and Maitland, puzzled, moved back on the ridge: but
the reason may have been that the news of Napoleon's deception was
sweeping along the line. Lieutenant Martin on the extreme right was
probably one of the first to recognise the Prussians. As the awful news
spread, 'everything suddenly gave way, men losing hope and giving up
... everyone knew it was all over.'[233] At that moment the Duke shouted
to Maitland's brigade to attack, 'now is your time', and as they poured
down the slope and across the valley, Colborne attacked from the right,
some Prussians joined in from the left, and the defenders of Hougoumont
turned on the rear through the retreating French.

Wellington himself stood up in his stirrups and waved his hat as the
prearranged signal for a general advance. He joined the charge, with
Rebécque beside him, and all the remaining line regiments, depleted
though they were (including the three battalions of Colonel Detmers)
followed. He urged them on, 'Don't give them time to rally. They won't
stand'. They didn't – it was 'sauve qui peut' as the great Armée du Nord,
broken and mauled, streamed south; Ney, who had had five horses killed
under him, desperately shouted to d'Erlon to stand fast, 'because if we
don't die here, the émigrés will hang us'. Ney did end before a firing
squad, but d'Erlon fled to exile in Munich, was granted an amnesty by
the Bourbons ten years later, and ended his career as Governor of Algeria.

As the remnants of the British cavalry joined the charge, they came up against two Guard battalions which had formed squares, in one of them Napoleon himself had apparently taken refuge; but they were bypassed; it was more "fun" (an actual quote) to continue the pursuit. Many of the French threw down their weapons and tried to surrender, pleading 'vive le Roi', but according to the bland aside of an officer of the 18th Hussars, 'It was too late, besides our men do not understand French'. Wounded men were trampled underfoot in the struggle to escape, others fell on their knees and simply waited either to be slaughtered or taken prisoner. Only one British battalion did not join the triumphant charge and stayed standing by the chaussée – it was the 27th Inniskillings, almost every man jammed dead in square.

Cavalié Mercer was characteristically sour. Another of Chassé's horse batteries, ordered up at the gallop, had unlimbered near him to open fire after a fierce barrage had reduced his troop to a tangled mass of broken guns, dead horses and wounded men. The recognition they got for saving his command from complete destruction was the following comment,

> These Belgians were all beastly drunk, and, when they first came up, not at all particular as to which way they fired, and it was only by keeping an eye on them that they were prevented from treating us and even one another. The wretches had probably done mischief elsewhere – who knows?[234]

Mercer's accusation is undermined by Gerard Rochell (he who had enjoyed cherries for breakfast). He wrote that they had received no alcohol that day since the woman who previously supplied them had gone missing.[235] However, historians tend to follow Mercer's line and refer (if at all) to Chassé's men as 'well refreshed by beer and genever', thus detracting from their achievement.

Van Omphal, who had been observing his old regiment, the Red Lancers, with whom he had served 'and counted many friends amongst them', had found himself at the head of the advance since he was on horseback, and came across Wellington, accompanied by Constant Rebècque. Rebècque later wrote that in this final charge, he had 'advanced into a hail of shot with Lord Wellington' and when his horse was shot through the skull covering him with a fountain of blood, 'je fus a même de me defender sabré a la main dans une melee du cavalerie' (*I had to defend myself sabre in hand in the midst of the cavalry*).[236]

The Duke ordered van Omphal to go to the Prussians whose twenty-gun battery, as they came up to the line, was actually causing havoc to Saxe-Weimar's defenders of Papelotte. The 4th Division of the French I Corps had been attacking the farmhouse all day, though in a fairly desultory way because of the difficult terrain and the lack of firm orders from Napoleon whose expectation of his IV Corps under Marshal Grouchy to arrive lasted until late afternoon. So Saxe-Weimar's greatest danger had come when the Prussians inflicted as many casualties in twenty minutes as he had suffered all day.

Van Omphal's was a hazardous assignment as the mingling of different elements (which had been a dangerous factor on occasion through the day) was now universal and 'more than once he had to wave his orange sash to prevent his being maltreated'.[237] He joined General Müffling, who had also been sent by Wellington to stage-manage the merger of the two armies, and an incensed Saxe-Weimar. For once, language was no bar to swift action as the three German speakers managed to contact von Ziethen; however, 'not knowing the Prince, [he] made no excuses and calmly replied, "my friend it is not my fault that your men look like French".'[238]

Over the whole field firing ceased but the smoke was so thick that nothing could be seen – men knew now there was a victory but, amazingly, could not be certain which side had been beaten. As the Prussians joined the reserve battalions on the ridge, Saxe-Weimar, back with his depleted troops,

> heard the fire of battle cease. I received a report that the battle had been won, the French pieces were there without horses and without men, and the enemy was trying to escape.[239]

Sergeant Robertson had found himself severely pressed and in command of two companies (two-thirds of his officers had been lost at Quatre Bras), and he was wondering how he could order a retreat pursued by cavalry over a mile of open field,

> I was aware it would be difficult to keep the men together, as they had never retreated before in similar circumstances.

Suddenly the Prussians were among them. The redcoats of the Highlanders avoided misunderstanding, and all somehow found the strength to burst into their national anthems. Constant Rebècque was the only officer fit to accompany Wellington off the field, and his multi-lingual journal records their conversation,

> En gallant le duc me dit, 'Well, what do you think of it?', je répond, 'I believe, sir, it is the finest thing you have ever achieved' et il ajouta, 'By God, I saved the battle four times myself.'[240]

This was no exaggeration. Wellington's conduct on 18 June was without doubt his finest hour; in Longford's words, 'his whole army had vibrated under his inspiration', and 'the eye could turn in no direction that it did not perceive him ... every ball... seemed fired at him and every gun aimed at him'.[241] 'The finger of Providence', to which he later paid tribute, was certainly upon him. Castlereagh paid tribute in Parliament on 22 June, 'The Duke was everywhere – at least where the danger was'. Napoleon's attempt to regain his Empire had failed, and Wellington had won a battle in which, as the veteran Harry Smith wrote, 'every moment was a crisis'.

CHAPTER 16

The Pursuit

NAPOLEON HAD DIRECTED his forces from a small knoll one and a half kilometres behind his front line, and it was near there – at an inn – that Blücher and Wellington met at nightfall and saluted each other in victory. The inn was called La Belle Alliance and the Prussians suggested that the day's battle should take that name – 'certainly not an improper denomination' as von Müffling put it.[242] Wellington made no comment but never considered the idea – the 'spin' of a British victory had already begun – though perhaps he was right: "la belle alliance" would be short-lived. For the moment, however, relations were cordial; it was decided that the road south would not permit both forces to hound the retreating French, and since Wellington admitted the allied army was 'fatigué à en mourir', Blücher volunteered the Prussians for the role.

Many of the exhausted British might have preferred the pursuit to the horrors of spending the night on the battlefield. Surrounded by corpses, the looters (often Belgian peasant farmers who reckoned it was one way of recouping their losses) and the thrashing movements of dying horses, they had no means to help the wounded who must wait until morning for rescue. Colonel Frederick Ponsonby of the Scots Greys lay for eighteen hours with, in addition to a punctured lung, two sabre wounds in his back.

Most of the veterans remembered an eerie silence – the effect on eardrums of the artillery barrages meant that it was often two or three days before they could hear clearly again. Under an almost full moon forty thousand dead and wounded men were sprawled in heaps over an area of little more than two miles by two and a half. Survivors described a scene that was 'calm and still'. The wounded lay among the stiffening dead, but few had the energy left to help them. More than ten thousand wounded horses still neighed and tried to scramble up on legs which had been shot away, (an infantry square threatened by cavalry, would aim low to bring the riders down.) Mercer found himself strangely incapable of putting these animals out of their misery, one near him, horribly mutilated, kept raising its head 'in a wistful gaze', but 'blood enough I had seen shed … and was sickened at the thought of shedding more'. The effort of firing a bullet between those glazing eyes seemed too much to ask of him.

Glittering in the moonlight were hundreds of cuirasses, alongside the drums which had beaten for the French advances and the high bearskins of the Imperial Guard. Over and above it all lay the stench of gunpowder and of death. Early in the morning fatigue parties were sent out to collect the wounded, but almost immediately the order came to march, and as the surgeons and wagons mostly followed the army south, some of the wounded faced many more days on the field before they could be carried back to Brussels.

Many of the Prussians were hardly less exhausted – beaten at Ligny, there had been no rest for them as they retreated north, and on the 18 June itself they had fought for many hours over twelve miles of appalling terrain. In addition, their supply train had been sent back to Louvain so they had had little food. Nevertheless, Blücher's iron resolve drove his men on, and what had been an orderly French retreat became a rout. "The great road" was littered with overturned wagons, as the sound of Prussian drums and bugles behind them caused panic, and men cut the traces to use the horses to escape. Sometimes a unit or two would turn to make a stand but were swept aside, attempted barricades were demolished by Prussian artillery, while in the villages when men dashed for shelter into the houses they were dragged out and despatched; in one village they set alight the barns of a farmhouse and burned alive the wounded who had been gathered there. Napoleon's secretary, Fleury de Chaboulon, recorded the Prussians'

> unparalleled barbarity. With the exception of a few experienced veterans, most of [our] soldiers had thrown away their arms and

found themselves defenceless; they were still massacred without pity.[243]

Occasionally they took prisoners but only with the intention of carrying out formal executions – one of these was Dominique Larrey, surgeon to the Imperial Guard and a man of Europe-wide reputation. As he was being led out to the firing squad a Prussian who had attended Larrey's lectures in Berlin, intervened and Larrey was released to return to Brussels where he assisted in treating casualties.

This 'paroxysm of ferocity', as Barbero terms it, can probably be attributed to the desperate fighting without quarter at both Ligny and Plancenoit (there is definite evidence that the French cut the throats of many prisoners) and the fact that Blücher, unlike Wellington, exerted little discipline on his men, rather encouraging them in their hectic revenge. Sergeant Wheeler of the 51st Regiment of Foot recorded the Prussian explanation,

> You English know nothing of the sufferings of war as we do. England has never been overrun by French armies as our country has, or you would act as we do.[244]

The great prize was Napoleon's carriage, captured just north of Genappe. Here the victors found quantities of jewels which he had not wished to leave in Paris, including diamonds worth a million francs, 300,000 francs in banknotes, his travelling case containing solid gold hairbrushes and mirrors and his seal-ring which found its way to Gneisenau's hand. Also left behind were copies of the proclamation he had intended to issue that night to the people of Belgium from the palace of Laeken: the English translation reads,

> The short-lived success of my enemies detached you for a moment from my Empire; in my exile on a rock in the sea I heard your complaints. ...Napoleon is amongst you ... rise in mass, join my invincible phalanxes to exterminate the remainder of those barbarians who are your enemies and mine: they fly with rage and despair in their hearts.

At Genappe, the village from which Saxe-Weimar had set out three days before, a narrow bridge blocked the fleeing French. The cavalry took to the fields, but the artillery was mostly abandoned on the road and the infantry crawled beneath the wagons in a desperate effort to avoid the ferocious pursuit. Further south they crossed the battlefield of Quatre Bras where the dead still lay rotting after three days of storm and sun. One of the few English prisoners whom they were determined to retain, later recalled with shame that his bare feet had found relief in treading on the softened corpses after the hardness of the stony road.

Wellington's acceptance of immediate pursuit suited the Prussians well. They were determined, if possible, to reach Paris first in order to gain the maximum political advantage, and consequently, men who had fought two major battles in five days were ruthlessly driven on a forced march for the next few days over difficult roads in blazing sun, often so far ahead of their supply wagons that no food was available. As they entered France they were likened to a swarm of locusts, 'they plunder and burn wherever they go and spare nothing', wrote a British veteran, 'the hatred that exists between the two nations is astonishing'.

The British troops had been allowed their night of fitful rest, before they thankfully left the battlefield behind them to join the pursuit, and they crossed the Belgian border by a western route through Binche late on 20 June. Saxe-Weimar complained of the Duke's

> brutality that he has used in relation with our chiefs, in accusing them of not knowing how to make their troops march, but without actually having taken care of assuring our subsistence.

Simultaneously, Wellington was railing against

> The troops of His Majesty the King of Holland [who] pillage and steal everywhere they go; even the headquarters, the house where I myself am staying, is not excluded.

One can choose whom to believe – Wellington's valid point was that fear of reprisals led to flight by villagers who might otherwise be a source of supply, though Saxe-Weimar's complaint raises the possibility that the Netherlanders were once more overlooked by the General Staff and Quartermasters. Corporal Wakker writes of three days of hunger, and refers to French meat as being so heavily spiced that 'wij hielden niet van dit' (*we did not like it*). Leonhard, the Nassauer, grumbled that they were

> forced to be the vanguard through all of France, with loaded muskets and fixed bayonets [suffering] hunger, thirst and all kinds of want.

The Prussians had their reasons, but British discipline held under Wellington's iron control. He was to issue a General Order as they entered France, reminding his troops of all nations that their sovereigns were allies of the King of France, and 'that France ought therefore be treated as a friendly country'. It was similar to the Orders he had issued in Portugal; Mercer grumbled that this was treating the former enemy 'as gentlemen', they should be given 'the punishment which France as a nation so richly deserves'.

As the Prussians stormed on south, following the retreating French, the roads Wellington took were inferior to theirs, but he encountered little resistance, and the two commanders met again on 23 June when their paths crossed. Here they agreed a joint march on Paris, and the Duke invited King Louis to join them at Cateau Cambrensis. Louis was in no hurry to risk his person since there were rumours of a French stand at Laon, halfway between the border and Paris. To ensure the King's safety from such a threat, the Duke launched an attack on the fortress of Cambrai which cost the lives of thirty men before its garrison surrendered, and Louis finally joined his liberators. Peronne, at the junction of the Somme and the Oise, offered fierce resistance and was taken 'by storm'; here Wellington accepted the French surrender and allowed the garrison troops to return to their homes.

He endeavoured to coordinate the dual advance at his slower pace since the importance of a British, rather than Prussian, domination of Paris had been impressed on him from London since at least the end of April. With definite information that the remnants of the French army under Soult and Grouchy were, indeed, concentrating near Laon, he agreed that the drive for the capital should be speeded up. However, Blücher once more pressed his exhausted men to greater effort, besieging the French fortresses he passed and leaving garrisons to control them, until he was at least forty kilometres ahead of the British.

Prussian atrocities continued, a private of the 11th Dragoons, following in their wake, described a village as 'a work of devastation', the chateau had been wrecked, 'not one article of furniture, from the costly pier glass to the common coffee-cup, which they had not smashed to atoms... and as to living things, there was none – not so much as a half-starved pigeon.' He continued, 'I was half ashamed of the connection between ourselves and the Prussians when I looked upon the horrid work they had perpetrated.'[245] Wellington apparently raised a similar concern about Prussian actions with Blücher, and simply received the same continental rebuff to British disapproval, 'My Lord Duke, the French were never in England.'

Wellington had summoned Prince Frederik who had spent 18 June out of the action with his ten thousand men at Hal, and they were now ordered to take the fortresses of Le Quesnoy and Valenciennes. The former fell quickly, and the Duke placed on record 'the intelligence and spirit with which this young Prince conducted this affair.' Valenciennes was a much tougher proposition, but after three days of bombardment, Wellington once more 'had great pleasure in reporting the good conduct of a battery of artillery of the troops of the Netherlands.'[246] Netherlanders were at last well trusted to be left in the rear on garrison duty. As they drew nearer to Paris Blücher suggested that the Belgian cavalry should undertake a night march to Pontoise, just northwest of Paris, 'where by the great similarity of language and uniform it might pass for French cavalry'. Wellington considered the idea and rejected it, but it was certainly a change from the former conviction that the opportunity of such similarity would be taken to change sides.

Meanwhile Grouchy had redeemed himself by a masterly withdrawal from Wavre; he and Vandamme at last ended their mutual hostility, though he had tactfully to reject an innovative plan by Vandamme to march west, capture Brussels, release the French prisoners there and drive King Willem back to Holland. They acted in unison, bringing fifty thousand men south for a possible renewal of hostilities. Blücher had diverted a Prussian corps from the pursuit to deal with Grouchy, but the French were able to enter and hold the Walloon town of Namur where, as a French colonel wrote,

> The inhabitants showed us every imaginable kindness … on all sides we hear words of concern for us, curses against the Prussians.

As the French left by the southern gate, the citizens defended the north one against Prussian attack until they were well on their way. Davout ordered Grouchy to join Soult at Laon; Soult had thirty thousand men there, but many were without weapons and the cavalry had lost most of their horses; consequently, 'men were disappearing in all directions'. The forces camped together at Soissons to await developments – two commanders who had found themselves ill-matched to the posts they were given: Grouchy, a great cavalry commander, weighed down with the cares of infantry and artillery, and Soult, a brilliant officer with experience against Wellington in the Peninsula, employed, not to manoeuvre on the field but to interpret Napoleon's often confusing orders.

Davout, charged with the defence of Paris, was in a strong strategic position as he flooded the river and canal north of St. Denis and destroyed the Seine bridge nearest to Malmaison (whether to protect Napoleon, who had retired there, from the Prussians or to prevent him from taking the field again is uncertain). However, with the quality and enthusiasm of his sizable force of troops and National Guardsmen doubtful, Davout wisely decided to keep Grouchy and Soult well away from Paris to avoid further bloodshed, though he was reluctant to surrender. In letters to both Wellington and Blücher he requested a cease-fire. From the former, he received the assurance,

> I have every reason on earth to stop the loss of blood by the brave troops I command … under conditions that assure the establishment and stability of the general peace.

But Blücher resisted, arguing that he need not observe a cease-fire simply because the French announced one. He wished to take Paris by storm (and one of his objectives was the destruction of the Pont d'Iena, to erase memory of the Prussian defeat in 1806 and French occupation of Berlin). He argued, ingenuously, that 'we want to enter Paris to protect decent citizens against the looting threatened by the mob,' (which "mob" was unspecified), and he warned Davout in his reply,

Only in Paris can there be a reliable cease-fire. We are pursuing victory, and God has given us both the means and the will to do it. Be careful my Lord Marshal of what you do.

The encirclement of Paris continued as the Prussians captured village after village in the southern suburbs, and the city finally capitulated on the evening of 3 July. Wellington rejected "the vain triumph" of a victorious parade, so it was left to Blücher to lead his army into the capital: four brigades – the infantry with fixed bayonets and the cavalry with drawn swords – marched to take up positions on all the islands and bridges of the Seine, as well as the Tuileries and the Louvre, while the reserve cavalry and artillery bivouacked on the Champs-Èlysées. Wellington stationed twenty thousand troops on the Bois de Boulogne.

Two days later the Prussians began laying explosive charges under the Pont d'Iena. With exquisite politeness Wellington contacted Blücher,

> I take the liberty of suggesting to you that you delay the destruction
> of the bridge ... until I can have the pleasure of seeing you tomorrow
> morning.[247]

He was able to persuade Blücher to delay his revenge until the other allied powers arrived in Paris to be consulted, well aware that they would refuse such a provocative act. In the meantime, he posted British guards on the bridge, trusting that the Prussians were unlikely to blow them up.

Napoleon had returned to Paris on horseback three days after the battle. According to the *Gentleman's Magazine*, he informed his ministers that 'his Army was no more and he required [their] assistance in the formation of another'. His nemesis, Joseph Fouché, whom he himself had appointed Minister of Police, ensured that the General Assembly of the government refused to support him, even when he offered to lead an army against the invaders as 'General Bonaparte'. He abdicated for the second time, appointing his young son, the four-year-old King of Rome, as his successor, and from Malmaison wrote an extraordinary appeal to the Prince Regent,

> Once more I am exposed to the factions which distract my country
> and to the enmity of the greatest powers of Europe, I have closed

my political career, and I come like Themistocles to throw myself upon the hospitality of the British people under the protection of their laws, which I claim from Your Royal Highness as the most powerful, the most constant and the most generous of my enemies.[248]

The able classicists in His Majesty's Government no doubt enjoyed the allusion to the commander at the Battle of Salamis who was then sent into exile, but, not surprisingly, they did not bother to reply.

The problem of Napoleon's future was a difficult one for the Allies, which they hoped others would solve; Lord Liverpool had declared, 'We wish that the King of France would hang or shoot Bonaparte, as the best termination of the business.' Blücher, too, argued for execution but Wellington, who, at Waterloo, had checked a sniper with Napoleon in his sights, was disgusted – he wrote to Charles Stuart, 'if the Sovereigns wished to put him to death they should appoint an executioner and it should not be me.'[249]

Napoleon himself now planned to go to America, and boarded a British battleship at Roquefort, confident of British protection. The ship first dropped anchor in Plymouth Sound where hundreds of small boats surrounded it, and it was feared that Bonaparte might escape to shore 'where no power could remove him'. He would show himself on the deck for some minutes at a time, declaring that not another "goutte de sang" would be shed on his account. The authorities were so jumpy that there were fatal accidents as the cutters and launches placed on guard rammed the sightseers. He and his suite were allowed to order any goods they required as long as they paid for them, and a billiard table, fine wines, books and chessmen were duly delivered to the ship.

After ten days, he was informed that he would be sent to St. Helena, despite his furious protest against 'this violation of my most sacred rights … the forcible disposal of my person and my liberty'. The island was the property the East India Company and thus outside both the rule of the British Crown, and, even more importantly, the jurisdiction of the English courts. As Paul O'Keefe points out, two hundred years later this would be termed "extraordinary rendition". Napoleon ended his life on that bleak, inhospitable, rat-infested island, eight hundred miles from land, guarded by Sir Hudson Lowe, 'the old fool' who, according to Wellington, 'could not read a map'.

CHAPTER 17

The Myth of Waterloo

It would be difficult now to conceive of any desirable addition to either the glory or the power of our happy Nation.[250]

THIS EXULTANT QUOTATION from *The Gentleman's Magazine* set the tone for the future. The Battle of Waterloo would enter myth and legend as one of the most illustrious achievements of British arms, confirming Britain's status as a Great Power and forming the foundation for her progress to imperial glory. It was the culmination of an extraordinary transformation – since 1783 a country on its knees then after the loss of America had established itself as Napoleon's only consistent adversary. In the intervening years as French armies marched in triumph through most of the cities of Europe, only Britain had opposed France, financially as well as militarily – Nelson and Wellington could be seen as European heroes also. The victory was universally recognised as a decisive turning-point, a moment which changed history, ushering in, for Britain at least, a period of peace and prosperity which gave her in the (perhaps slightly exaggerated) words of Rory Muir 'a sense of uniqueness, an inner confidence which lasted a full century until it was shattered on the Somme' just over a year after the hundredth anniversary. Even a French historian was to admit that 'on that day the perspective of the human race was altered. Waterloo is the hinge of the nineteenth century'.

Streets, public buildings, bridges, railway stations, even children, were named for the great battle. Every year church bells rang from dawn till dusk on 18 June, and survivors were guaranteed an admiring audience well into old age. The Rector of the Suffolk town of Framlingham offered a freehold farm to the Battle's most courageous non-commissioned officer – awarded to a sergeant of the Coldstream Guards. Poets and artists endeavoured, with varying success, to immortalise the struggle, and as the veterans leapt into print, interest never flagged. Rhetoric soared to ever more dizzy heights:

> The French have felt, the world has seen, and posterity will know that England's sons are best in the fight … [England] alone has assisted all and held her own head high without assistance.

"The Great Duke" himself was seen as a powerful symbol of Britain's transformation in the world – as he lived on for nearly forty years, even a political career of variable success did not lessen the reverence in which he was held. Sir William Fraser, eighty years later, wrote of Wellington's 'guiding spirit in the Greatest Battle the world has ever known'; Elizabeth Longford quotes another eye-witness at Waterloo,

> [Wellington's] entire concentrated attention, exclusive aim and intense thought were devoted impartially, imperturbably, and grandly to the Whole, the All.

Disraeli's funeral oration in 1852 referred to his fifteen victories, crowned by the one 'that gives a colour and a form to history.'

However, the development of the Waterloo myth demanded a dramatic simplification of the narrative – the elimination of anything or anyone which might detract from this glorious achievement of British military strength and the veneration of the man who embodied it: the title of this book shows just how successful the process has been.

Prussia's contribution was initially recognised: Blücher was invited to England in 1816 to receive a formal acknowledgement from the British government of his role; according to Cornwell, he surveyed London from Blackheath and characteristically remarked, 'what a city to sack'. But soon enough amnesia set in, and it became the accepted wisdom that the battle was already won before the Prussians' late arrival on the scene.

Many of the recollections of veterans simply fed 'the Myth'. As Keegan has pointed out, few of them could ever have been aware, as gunpowder smoke hung like a cloud over the entire area, of anything beyond their few yards of vision and the movement of those closest to them. Graphic and poignant descriptions revealed great courage but were often contradictory, essentially the experiences of individuals whose attitudes and assumptions before the Campaign would now be perpetuated. They recorded what they saw – Netherlanders in full retreat at both Quatre Bras and Waterloo – they often had little knowledge of the cause and did not care enough to find out. It is significant that the veterans describe the cavalry charges in great detail and their descriptions nearly always correspond – it was only when the artillery barrages ceased, the smoke lifted and the squares watched and waited, could any impression of the wider field be gained. Elsewhere there could be nothing more than "a worm's eye view".

Some warning voices were raised against anti-foreign prejudice. Macready, whose regiment had been reprieved by Chassé, clashed furiously with Siborne to the extent that there were rumours of a duel, and he specifically praised van Merlen 'no braver soldier [was] among those lost at Waterloo'. Van Merlen's reputation – perhaps as "an English gentleman" with a sense of honour – was burnished by a story recounted by Christopher Summerville, that when he had a French general at his mercy, he told him,

> This is my side of the battlefield, yours is over there. Take care of yourself and farewell.

Major Dawson Kelly, formerly of the 73rd, struck a note of caution in his correspondence with Siborne,

> It is fully within my memory that the fog and smoke lay so heavily on the ground that we could only ascertain the approach of the enemy by the noise and clashing of arms …and it has often occurred to me that the accuracy and particulars with which the *Crisis* has been so frequently and minutely described must have had a good deal of fantasy in the narrative.[251]

While Sir George de Lacy Evans, to whom Siborne complained of the difficulty of reconciling different accounts (a problem for historians ever since), assured him that this was entirely to be expected,

There is scarcely an instance, I think, of two persons even though only fifty yards distant from each other, who give of such events a concurring account.

There were disagreements between the commanders themselves: Hew Halkett's account of the capture of the French general Cambronne in the closing stages of Waterloo, was contested by Hussey Vivian,

Where the devil General Halkett [he was actually a Colonel] found twelve or fourteen guns of the Guard in full play after he had witnessed an attack of Hussars on a square of infantry, I am quite at a loss to imagine.[252]

It may be that Halkett was in the right – Vivian had a reputation for self-aggrandisement: he once boasted that he, personally, had by his final (and only) charge 'turned the fate of the day'. The recipient of this confidence remarked that

The place he charged was two miles out of position and half an hour after the enemy retreated.

Wellington's decision to remain above the fray meant that he steadfastly refused any appeal for the clarity which he alone might be expected to provide. Argument and debate continued to surround the campaign as every British officer took to the pages of Colburne's *United Services Magazine*, to claim that his regiment alone clinched victory; the Duke replied to one amateur historian,

The history of a battle is not unlike the history of a ball. Some individuals may recall all the little events of which the great result is the battle won or lost, but no individual can recall the order in which ... they occurred which makes all the difference

And he continues with a very significant line of reasoning,

You cannot write a true history of a battle without including the faults and misbehaviour of part at least of those engaged. Believe me, that every man you see in a military uniform is not a hero ... it is better for the general interests to leave those parts of the story untold than to tell the whole truth.[253]

One can wonder what lay behind this frank assessment. Hofschröer argues at forensic length in *The Smallest Victory*, that Wellington was determined, above all, to protect his own reputation, and that he was as ruthless in dealing with dissent as he had been during his military career. It is possible that he viewed this less as a personal issue but more as a national one. He was well aware that he had become a symbol in which the personal and the national interest overlapped; any diminution of his role could affect the very status of Britain herself and sap that 'inner confidence'. As Hofschröer points out, Wellington certainly 'airbrushed' the Prussian role. Prussian territorial ambition was increasingly seen as the next threat to Europe's balance of power, and without the mutual trust between him and Blücher, the dangerous clash between Britain and Prussia at the Congress of Vienna in early 1815 over control of the minor German states might well have undermined the whole coalition against Napoleon.

It was far easier to simplify the narrative where the Netherlanders were concerned, and that success has lasted almost to this day. Few of the British veterans even mentioned foreign troops except to vilify them: Mercer's highly readable memoirs were the basis of much mis-information, and Private Wheeler of the 51st Foot was not far behind given his interpretation of the chaos at Nivelles on 16/17 June as troops scrambled from their far-flung posts to join the Allied Army,

> The place was crowded with heavy cavalry belonging to Belgium... we halted to let them pass, but afterward found they were running away, helter-skelter, the Devil take the hindmost ... they were the rankest cowards that ever formed part of an army.

It is a confirmed fact that this cavalry had been ordered speedily up to Mont Saint Jean to form the advance guard as a concentration point for the rest of the army. These two – Wheeler and Mercer – could, at least, be said to be describing what they actually saw, even if their understanding was at fault; they are thus less guilty than those who deliberately set out to deceive or conceal.

The Netherlands veterans were proud of their achievement and watched with bewilderment and growing anger as 'Engeland's roem to vermeerderen ten koste van de eer van andere volkeren' (*England's fame was magnified at the cost of the honour of other nations*). As time wore on and historians joined the fray, there was still no divergence from the determined conviction of foreign incompetence. At the very end of the nineteenth century, Herbert Maxwell raised the vexed question of the Duke's strategic hesitancy which, he realised, had left the Netherlanders so exposed at Quatre Bras;

> It is scarcely to the credit of our English historians that [so] much has been said uncomplimentary to our Belgian-Dutch allies.

Oman, the leading Napoleonic historian, launched a fierce attack on 'Maxwell's curious mental attitude', asserting that the Dutch-Belgians 'gave their allies the gravest cause for dissatisfaction'. Veneration for the Duke can lead modern historians, also, into the most biased and sycophantic contortions,

> Wellington was fortunate that the artillery and sharpshooter ordeal came to an end fairly quickly, although if it had not he would probably have thought of a move to counter it.[254]

Veterans and historians alike reveal their prejudice in the choice of language: there were many 'movements to the rear'. When they refer to the British they are usually seen as 'temporary retirements to regroup'; but when applied to the Netherlanders they are 'a panic-stricken flight' which the sources assume to be permanent, and, most probably, a prelude to looting. British instances are suppressed: Andrew Barnard of the Rifles wrote three days after the battle as he lay wounded:

> I regret to say that a great number of our men went to the rear without cause after the appearance of the Cuirassiers ... this vexes me very much as it is the first time such a thing has ever happened in the regiment.[255]

Once he had recovered, it was never mentioned again, although, as Urban immediately points out, Wellington himself had recognised that 'all soldiers ran away sometimes, it was just a matter of how quickly they came back' – and most of the Netherlanders did. Their artillery batteries, for example, continually had to strip the harness from dead horses while under fire, haul the guns back through the wounded and the dead to repair the damage, piece together the tack and return to the line: no troops could ever be spared for their defence. All sides in the conflict use equivocal language to conceal or adjust situations to protect their reputation – 'the sunken road' marking the British battle-line was actually an easy in-and-out leap for a horse, but for the French cavalry who came to grief there it was remembered as a steep ravine – 'the Valley of Death', and enthusiastic artists emphasised the drama.

Linguistic implications are an important element in the study of the Waterloo campaign, and the British reluctance to move outside their own language has led to grave misrepresentation. Even the German studies (more accessible than the Dutch) have only recently been taken into account: Hofschröer gets an English translation, and his description of the horrendous difficulties which the Prussians had to overcome on 18 June as they came to Wellington's aid, explains the late arrival which has previously puzzled many historians; one account even asserted the Prussian delay was due to lazy staff-work.

The reasons for such lack of acknowledgement of the foreign troops extend, of course, well beyond mere linguistics. The most charitable one is simple misunderstanding: both of the logistical problems with which the Netherlanders had to contend, and of their contribution to the campaign. With the exception of Baring at La Haie Sainte, few British troops seem to have experienced the ammunition shortage, equipment deficiency or lack of subsistence which is recorded again and again in Dutch-Belgian accounts. The British cavalry lost many horses and this is accepted without question as a reason for the ominous category of 'missing'; the Netherlands cavalry are blamed for reluctance or absence, but they had no reserve mounts at all, and were powerless without them.

The £2 million British subsidy proved totally inadequate to supply the soldiers of the Netherlands army with even the most basic equipment they needed. Weapons of different calibre were issued almost at random, with no certainty that the nearest supply wagons would be carrying the correct ammunition. These wagons were, too often, as Colonel Reuther reported to the King, serviced by men and horses unfit for the role with some of the animals even unbroken; bolting horses could overturn powder wagons, causing massive explosions and badly affecting other contingents. The small area of the battlefield of Waterloo (two miles by two and a half)

Fig. 7: Allegory of the Heroes (Rijksmuseum, Amsterdam FMH6059-B) C van Waard

meant that even those willing to brave the line were hampered by the sheer weight of traffic. The supply road was littered with broken down vehicles, columns of prisoners and lines of wounded, so very few ammunition wagons could reach their objective. With hardly any sappers of their own and the departure of the British ones, the Netherlands artillery teams, issued with only enough ammunition for one barrage, were often forced to withdraw some distance along the crowded road, not for flight, but in order to hunt for supplies; Rebècque himself had to leave the field at one point to find the right cartridges for the 2nd Division.

Through the nineteenth century Dutch historians recorded their country's achievement at Quatre Bras and Waterloo, and many prints portrayed it in the traditional form – the print of the Allegory of the Heroes shows the Prince's place of honour which he never lost. However they could never make their voices heard in England; only historians of the seventeenth century Dutch Golden Age have ever been granted an English translation. Dutch militarism, never an important trait, had had its brief flowering then, when under the ruling Orange stadhouders, their very small country had been a leading power in Europe. Especially after the final split of the joint monarchy in 1839 both Belgium and Holland were content to relinquish any military significance and pursue their colonial interests in perhaps fortuitous obscurity.

Increasingly the Dutch accepted such anonymity, with only occasional protest; one of the most recent actually dared to attack Simon Schama whose support for the eighteenth century "patriots" showed

> zoveel rancune jegens de Oranjes dat mijn haren recht overeind gaan staan (*so much rancour against the Oranges that my hair stood on end*).

and he protests that the reference comes in the only chapter of the book without notes.[256]

CHAPTER 18

Concealment

THE NEED FOR simplification to create the 'myth of Waterloo' led Britain inexorably through the nineteenth century into a state of mind where emotional coherence triumphed over historical accuracy. The prophecy of a contributor to *The United Services Journal* was fulfilled,

> Some errors obtain such possession of people's minds that it is extremely difficult to root them out, and, in consequence, they are sometimes transmitted from age to age as established truths.

National pride, the memories of veterans, Wellington himself and English-speaking historians all played a part in the establishment of a myth-system, and all four are relevant also to the concealment of foreign achievement. The Netherlanders would, understandably, have no place in the myth, but the treatment of them went beyond simply the suppression 'of what clashes with or diminishes myth' – there was a further veneer of quite deliberate denigration. Sir William Napier in his six-volume history of the Peninsular Campaign, published in the last years of the nineteenth century, was probably fully aware of this,

> Depend upon it, Waterloo has a long history of secret politics attached to it, which will not be made known in our days, if ever.

National distortion began early with a panorama of the battle, displayed in Leicester Square in 1816, a Dutch visitor noted, people approached as if to a holy shrine; it was, he said, as if 'geene Nederlanders eenig belangrijk deel gehad' (*not a single Netherlander had played an important part*). In the panorama displayed in Amsterdam the same year, the British generals, Picton, Ponsonby and Vivian 'in vollen luister pralen' (*shine in full glory*), and the true heroism of every combatant was acknowledged. Jeroen van Zanten in his biography of the later King Willem II (the Prince of Orange), describes the London panorama as 'riekte naar geschieds vervalsing' (*reeking of falsified history*).

William Tomkinson, who had remarked on 'the moustachioed countenances' of the foreigners, was happy enough to embroider his account of Quatre Bras, 'the Dutch-Belgians did not behave well' and when they left the field 'commenced plundering in the rear, their cavalry attacking batmen in charge of the baggage'. The cavalry was almost certainly too mauled to do any such thing, but since Tomkinson, by his own account, was still bravely on the field, he could not possibly know what was happening behind the line. Imagination or malice also played a part in a description of 'hundreds [sic] of deserting Dutch and Belgian cavalry' *before* Ney's cavalry attack at Waterloo. It is more likely that these were the survivors of Uxbridge's charge since the successful actions of Ghingy and of Trip (both of whom remained on the field) represented, at that stage, the only Netherlands cavalry in action. A charitable assessment might endorse the account of another veteran,

> In truth every part of a field of battle must differ markedly and so must the account of every one engaged, and still all may be firmly persuaded of the truth of the statements they make.

One example of this is a curious account in an 1865 memoir by a Dutch veteran. He describes an incident late on 18 June when he saw an officer of the French cuirassiers repeatedly riding forward to stand staring at the ridge; three times he returned to his unit, but then, finally, spurred his horse to a gallop, straight at the Allied centre:

> 'zijnen sabel opsteken en een witte doek van onder zijn kurass trekken'
> (*his sabre raised and drawing a white cloth from under his cuirass*)[257]

He was apparently conducted to Wellington by the Nassauer, Colonel Thielen, but then returned to his unit, so it could not be a further example of the desertions which certainly occurred at intervals through the day; it has been suggested that the man issued a warning of the imminent Imperial Guard advance. The account does not seem to appear in any English work though such action could hardly remain unnoticed, but it would be a strange thing to invent.

Mercer's accusation of cowardice after Quatre Bras is but one example of a frequently voiced complaint that too many men accompanied their wounded comrades off the field. The French had pioneered wagons on which rough litters could be loaded to take the wounded to the rear; for the Allied Army there were only blankets which needed at least three fit men as carriers, and the medical facilities were well behind the line. It was easy to accuse the "Dutch-Belgians" of seizing the opportunity to "desert". However, Lieutenant Basil Jackson of the Staff Corps, does refer to 'the good nature of the Dutch drivers' when he met a 12-pounder Netherlands gun-carriage labouring north after Quatre Bras, on which were clustered about a dozen wounded men, English as well as Dutch.[258]

A further problem for allied commanders was the return to Brussels on 18 June, while fighting still continued, of two thousand prisoners. Perponcher was directly ordered to provide four hundred infantry for the escort of these (undoubtedly because French speakers were advisable to control them); but this was never public knowledge. The worst conclusion could be drawn about their disappearance: John Kincaid of the Rifles noted 'the number of vacant spots that were left nearly along the whole line, where a great part of the dark dressed foreign troops had stood,' the assumption was, of course, desertion of that element which had been viewed with such suspicion before the Campaign.

Clayton quotes a veteran's account of Belgians 'deserting their standards',

> The road was thronged with Belgian fugitives in whole companies both horse and foot, intermingled with many wounded officers and soldiers …

Battle accounts are full of descriptions of the wounded returning up the road to Brussels and often deserters also (of every nationality) but, significantly, this one continues, 'together with numerous prisoners of all ranks and sorts'; that is, *French* prisoners, and arguably, the ones for which Perponcher was providing escorts.[259]

Wellington's treatment of Baron David Chassé must be seen as dishonest. He refused to allow his earlier antagonism and doubts to be dispelled by Chassé's action on the field. It is certainly arguable (and not only by reading the Dutch accounts) that this action was crucial, but he was to receive no recognition. On 5 July, having seen Wellington's first dispatch, the Baron wrote ('tactfully' as he himself put it) to his commanding officer Lord Hill,

> there was no mention of my division whatsoever. I presume that its conduct eluded Your Excellency's attention when writing your report to the Duke.[260]

Hill's reply on 11 July offered little consolation: his report had reached the Duke 'too late to be recorded', although this "report" was actually a letter to Wellington dated 20 June, drawing to his attention 'the steady conduct of the 3rd Division of the troops of the Netherlands under the command of Major-General Chassé'. Even Hill, possibly Wellington's most valued commander, was unable to influence any dispatch and could only offer the soothing assurance,

> that His Grace is aware of the fine conduct of the troops under your command on the glorious day, and … that it will always be my greatest pleasure to vouch for it.

Hill had been wounded earlier when he was caught in crossfire and his horse went down, so he must have been prompted by those he trusted to write as he did. It would have been for Wellington who had obviously been in the sector which witnessed the final charge, to acknowledge Chassé's contribution: this he never did. Just possibly, he might not have identified his foreign troops during the chaos, but it seems yet another example of Saxe-Weimar's complaint about

> The very little due recognition the Duke of Wellington rendered in official reports … the late and cold manner in which the decorations of the Order of Willem were distributed, and the near total lack of judgement that he showed in the distribution.[261]

Wellington's main dispatch, written the day after the battle by an exhausted man, depressed by the scale of the casualties and loss of so many friends, is an extraordinary achievement in its detailed record of the battle, but he was later to admit, 'I should have given more praise'. However he never intervened afterwards to correct prejudice or injustice. The only Netherlander he acknowledges is Trip, and it is a moot point that his mention of 'General Vanhope' (as discussed in Chapter 14) was a concealment of Chassé's name.

Alert observers were, at a very early stage, critical of Wellington's dispatch – he did not tell the whole truth, and John James, the assistant surgeon, accuses him of censorship if for good reason. He wrote from Paris (sent by separate courier),

> Half the letters from the army do not go, but are probably overhauled by clerks as the Duke of Wellington is not a little disposed to repress all strictures on his conduct … there are many things omitted … for good reasons they are suppressed.[262]

The Waterloo Dispatch was praised by some for its 'noble simplicity, perfect calmness and exemplary modesty', but they were in the minority; most of the British public searched in vain for more detailed descriptions of regimental and personal achievements. Lord Uxbridge's sister even termed the dispatch "odious", though he might not have come well out of a fuller account – she may have perceived irony in the description of his "protective" role in the 17 June retreat, described by Mercer as 'wild and confused'. Wellington carefully referred to it as an occasion 'upon which his Lordship has declared himself to be well satisfied …'.

One of the most curious strands in British sources is the treatment of the Prince of Orange himself which sometimes appears almost manic. Many commentators suffer from attacks of adjectival hysteria – ignorant, conceited, crass, incompetent, useless, callow, stupid, asinine, inexperienced, (and a new one, recently, from an otherwise brilliant book, wilful) – an over-promoted idiot, 'out of his depth', a man whose wounding was a relief to Wellington and his own men alike. Only Rory Muir goes against the tide – obliging, brave and willing.

The early memoirs of British veterans seldom mention the Prince, with the significant exception of the siege of Badajoz and its aftermath when he was Wellington's chosen companion to enter the rioting city, while Dutch veterans like Corporal Wakker reveal a very different man. The Duke is certainly blameless here; he maintained friendly contact with the Prince, writing to him later that year as Willem travelled to St. Petersburg to marry the daughter of the Tsar: 'I assure Your Royal Highness that you made an impression on all those who had the satisfaction to be near you [in] the past years and events.' Cynics might detect irony there too, but whenever Willem visited London, either as Prince or King, he would be invited to dine at Apsley House and there seems to have been genuine warmth in the relationship. After the Prince's two undoubted errors have been clarified, one is left with the abstract accusations of "youthful recklessness and inept command". The first of these shows that, if true, he was not the only one. Plenty of veterans recalled with amazement the actions they had performed at the height of battle. Uxbridge, on his own admission, behaved recklessly; an officer in the 16th Light Dragoons wrote afterwards

> I think the result to the Duke must be that Lord Uxbridge is too young a soldier to be much relied on with a separate command from a feeling that he will risk much in a desire to do something.[263]

This 'young soldier' was forty-seven.

The failure of the British cavalry at Waterloo was certainly hinted at in English sources – the report of the funeral of Sir William Ponsonby of the Union Brigade, reads,

> It is said (but we hope untruly) that he lost his life in consequence of the indiscreet valour of two of his regiments who continued a pursuit nearly two miles beyond the infantry ... while restraining their rashness he fell.[264]

As regards the Prince's command performance he personally ensured the success of the desperate two-hour initial defence of the Quatre Bras crossroads, and he was placed in the centre of Wellington's line on the plateau of Mont St. Jean. Van der Capellan reported to King Willem that he had been told by the Duke that the Prince had directed the action so well that there had been no need to send him further orders.

Fig. 8: Prince of Orange (Royal Archive, The Hague PR/0687) Willem Grebner, 1816

It is perhaps significant that the chorus of personal abuse against the Prince only begins to appear after his death (and that of Wellington three years later). That abuse has gathered momentum, and many of the adjectives above appear in the recent studies which have otherwise offered valuable clarification and explanation in addition to graphic narrative and, sometimes, even the overdue acknowledgement of the men he led. The Prince returned to Holland to be hailed as "Held (*Hero*) van Waterloo", and he has as much right to that title as many others – he made mistakes certainly, but one could adapt the comment of Vels Heijn, what commander 'had on that record a clean slate?' The print (from 1816) reveals a handsome and intelligent face, his hand resting on a cannon and the sling a reminder of his injury – the rhyming inscription roughly reads,

> May you in Netherland, rue Prince Willem's wound,
> Had his blood not flowed, in shackles you were bound.

The reason for British animosity is hard to fathom. The Lion Monument at Waterloo to mark the Prince's contribution certainly upset topographers since to achieve its height the ground round the sunken road at Mont Saint Jean was lowered – the Duke complained, 'they have ruined my battlefield'. But still the sheer unreferenced malice here is strange; returning drunk from a race meeting is hardly unknown, and allied foreign commanders in other wars have never been immune from criticism. It is the ultimate example of the dictionary definition of "concealment" – the suppression of truth or known fact, to the injury or prejudice of another. One does not need to delve too deeply into the chequered British relationship with the Benelux countries to be aware of an arrogance and lack of understanding which can be manifest today. On the other hand, perhaps this should simply join the other perplexing features which honest historians admit they cannot explain.

Very gradually through the twentieth century, historians began to question the approved wisdom. Elizabeth Longford's magisterial work is more generous to the Netherlanders since she is one of the few "buitenlanders" to have been granted access to the Koninklijk Huisarchief. In 1993 David Hamilton Williams was able to access documents there through the translation of Nicolaas Vels Heijn, and his work with its voluminous references and notes began, at last, to ensure that the contradictions, inconsistencies and injustice which the purely personal accounts reveal can no longer be ignored. Not before time 'the hidden heroes' are emerging from the shadows.

CHAPTER 19

Aftermath – the Netherlands

I N THE NETHERLANDS the Waterloo Campaign was seen as confirmation of the revival of monarchy. The House of Orange-Nassau
had always flourished at times of war and crisis. In the early years
of the eighteenth century Prince Johan Willem Friso of Orange had
commanded troops against the French under the Duke of Marlborough;
now, once more, a Prince of Orange had served as second-in-command
to a British military genius in the defeat of Bonaparte. A letter from Lord
Bathurst, the War Minister, to Wellington on 24 June 1815 acknowledged
both the parallel, and also some pleasure that the British diplomacy at
Vienna seemed to have been vindicated,

> Your Grace will be pleased to convey to General His Royal Highness
> the Prince of Orange, the satisfaction the Prince Regent has expressed
> in observing that in the actions of the 16th and 18th inst., His Royal
> Highness has given an early proof of those military talents for which
> his ancestors have been renowned, and that by freely shedding his
> blood in defence of the Netherlands he has cemented a union of
> the people of the House of Orange, which it is to be hoped will
> become thereby indissoluble.[265]

The victory ensured the survival of this joint monarchy for longer than
even the most optimistic observers had predicted, as it became a powerful

symbol of the new regime, and also a badly needed element of cohesion. The churches of both Protestant Holland and Catholic Belgium joined in thanksgiving, and 18 June was observed as an official holiday through the 1820s. The Dutch, especially, but also the Belgians, despite their ambivalent attitude towards France, had suffered severely through the Napoleonic years, and the union held.

Belgium had, in the summer of 1815, proved herself, 'a sister of charity to war-torn Europe' as the citizens threw open their homes to serve as hospitals medical supplies were rushed to the city and local civilian doctors joined medical men summoned from London in dealing with the thousands of wounded. Wellington wrote a heartfelt letter to the burgermeester two months later,

> I did not expect the tender care, the kindness, which the inhabitants have displayed towards us, and I beg you to believe, and to let them know, that their conduct has made upon us all an impression which will never be effaced from our memory.

The nature of the terrain – woodland and still plenty of standing rye – meant that even ten days later living men were being discovered, though by that time few could be saved since gangrene had spread through shattered limbs. One British cavalry officer was found with a sword in the upper thigh through the wood and leather of his saddle and into the dead horse – a surgeon had to separate them where he lay. Amputation was almost the automatic treatment by British surgeons; the rumour that French doctors took huge risks to avoid such maiming simply because it would mean that men became a burden on the state, seems to have originated with the xenophobic William Tomkinson, but as John Davy, a hospital assistant, admitted, 'most of the operations such as amputation of the thigh proved fatal'; unsurprisingly, officers fared best: Uxbridge and Fitzroy Somerset underwent amputation and survived.

The Belgian peasants, although guilty of looting after the battle from the wounded as well as the dead, at least played their part in the massive task of burial. There were so many corpses at Hougoumont that, unusually, pyres were lit. Elsewhere, trenches were dug but at only two spades deep, weather and erosion would soon reveal limbs, and even faces, to the horrified gaze of the many visitors to the battlefield later that summer, although they also noted hundreds of scarlet poppies flowering over the fields.

Löben Sels' assembly of the recollections of officers during the 1830s, by means of detailed questioning in a similar format to that used by Siborne, was never published, but remained in his private family archive. Although there is no indication of their origin, the fact that some reply in French and some in Dutch would seem to indicate that they include Belgians, and they have been made available by translations commissioned by John Franklin. Some of the correspondence shows great bitterness about the lack of recognition they had received. Saxe-Weimar was the most forceful in his response of 29 August 1841,

> You may have noticed, my dear captain, that the officers … who served in the campaign of 1815 do not like to discuss it, the memory … leaves us as cold as a review of the camp in Beyen… All those who participated remember the character and the manner in which our poor army was organised, administered and rewarded at that time.[266]

He seems, here, to be blaming King Willem as much as the British; Willem had certainly made many enemies in the intervening years (and had, in fact, abdicated the year before). Saxe-Weimar remained in the army, commanding a Dutch Division against the French in Belgium in 1831, and the rather grim print shows this large man at the age of fifty-five when he was commanding Dutch forces in the East Indies where his health broke down. He maintained a regular and respectful correspondence with the Prince, though sometimes with oblique references which seem to criticise the King. Both men lost much-loved sons in their twenties and the letters of commiseration in the Huisarchief show real affection.

In 1830 the six-year reign in France of Charles X, brother of Louis XVIII, was ended by the "July revolution", and, as before, French upheaval spilt over into a receptive Belgium which had continued to fret under Dutch rule. King Willem's "far-reaching meddling" had already antagonised his southern subjects: the origin of the term "double Dutch" being his decree that the vote of a Dutchman was worth two of a Belgian's. The Prince travelled to Brussels as negotiator since his reputation there was a great deal better than his father's. His efforts initially resulted in a compromise, the Treaty of XVIII Articles, agreed by the European powers,

BERNHARD.

HERTOG VAN SAXE WEIMAR.

Amsterdam by H. Moolenyzer.

Fig. 9: Prince Bernard of Saxe-Weimar (Rijksmuseum Amsterdam RP-P-1905-5295)

but when it was sent to his father for ratification Willem flatly rejected it, though it is unlikely, anyway, that Belgium would have accepted it.

A Dutch gunboat, patrolling the Scheldt, was blown by contrary winds into Antwerp where it was boarded by a group of hostile Belgians. Its commander, one Jan van Speijk, responded somewhat dramatically by blowing up the boat, himself, his crew and most of the attackers. In the autumn of 1832 a French force crossed the Belgian frontier to assist their "fellow revolutionaries", and David Chassé, still in Dutch service at the age of sixty-six, defended Antwerp against French siege until he was finally forced to surrender to the same General Gérard who had tried on 18 June to persuade Grouchy to march towards the sound of gunfire. His letter to Löben Sels apologises for the fact that the maps he had drawn of the 1815 Campaign 'were lost by a fatality during the revolt in Belgium'. The French (and Dutch) armies withdrew, but sporadic outbreaks of rebellion marked the next seven years, during a de facto acceptance of the breakup of the joint monarchy.

The Chamber of Deputies in Brussels (containing Wellington's supposed Bonapartists) were requested by "the French party" to destroy the Lion Monument on the field of Waterloo; they argued that it was a symbol of "their" defeat, and it should be converted into bombs and

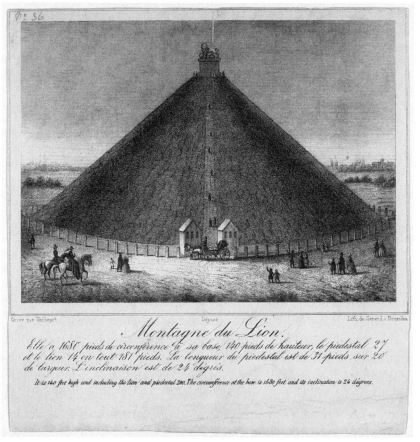

Fig. 10: Lion Monument, Waterloo (Rijksmuseum, Amsterdam FMH6050-B) H. Gérard

bullets 'to defend the liberty and independence of the two peoples [i.e. Belgium and France]'. The monument had already greatly annoyed Wellington since its considerable height was achieved by destruction of the banks of the sunken road; most people, fulfilling the line of argument in this study, assume it is the British lion, not the Batavian one.

It can be imagined that these proceedings were watched with smug satisfaction in London – pre-Campaign conviction was finally validated. The move for destruction was defeated however, partly by a petition from the villagers of Mont Saint Jean and Waterloo who were benefitting mightily from tourism, while a wider argument was the valid one that without the Campaign, Belgium would still be a département of France. It was also important not to antagonise the European powers, and eventually the softly-softly approach triumphed: by the Treaty of London in 1839, Belgian independence was guaranteed by the Concert of Europe, the United Kingdom [sic] of the Netherlands and the Kingdom of Belgium. A suggestion that the son of Louis Philippe, now Citizen-King of France, should take the newly created crown was, however, a step too far, and Prince Leopold of Saxe-Coburg-Gotha (previously married to Princess Charlotte) became King of Belgium.

This seemingly minor treaty concerning a country of little importance was, seventy-five years later, to assume enormous significance. It was Britain, as usual thinking of Antwerp, who insisted in 1839 that not only the independence, but also the neutrality of Belgium must be guaranteed. In 1914 the German invasion was held to violate that neutrality, and Britain went to war on what the German Chancellor von Bethmann-Hollweg, termed 'a mere scrap of paper'.

King Willem had made himself so unpopular that his marriage, three years after the death of his very popular wife, to a Belgian Catholic countess, forced his abdication at the age of seventy-one. His family relationships, too, were often fraught. A Dutch historian quotes an extraordinary letter written by the Prince's Russian wife a few years after Waterloo. Grand Duchess Anna Pavlovna writes to her mother Maria Feodorovna about a meeting she has recently had with her father-in-law,

> Hij zei me dat Willem een ontaarde zon was … ik zal ervoor zorgen dat deze driftkop geen enkele macht meer heeft.

(*he told me that Willem was a degenerate son* [and that he] *will now take care that this hothead remains powerless.*)

Anna continues, obviously relating the conversation verbatim, that the King told her it was a power-struggle, one or other of them would have to go under, that Willem was a bad soldier and a bad general. She attempts to defend her husband by recalling his courage at Waterloo, but this is dismissed,

Ja, zei hij, dat is waar, maar hij had geluk dat hij gewond raakte want anders zou hij zijn verslagen.

(*Yes, he said, that is true but he had the good fortune to be wounded for otherwise he would have been defeated.*)[267]

The British could hardly have done a better demolition job on the Prince than this tirade from his own father to whom he had written so happily after the battle. The relationship between them worsened dramatically as time went on, whether from the elder man's political misjudgements, his jealousy of a military career more successful than his own ignominious one, or, simply, the usual tensions between ruler and heir.

The Prince succeeded his father after the abdication, and his short reign of eight years was a relatively successful one. He stabilised the public finances and achieved the country's first surplus in seventy years by further developing various colonial ventures. As revolution again swept Europe in 1848, he acted quickly to introduce a new more liberal constitution, which would ensure the monarchy's future (although his son would again endanger it); of the first three Kings of the Netherlands, he was by far the most popular and he was genuinely mourned.

Conclusion

I N THE LETTER to his brother William, written the day after the battle, Wellington wrote with searing honesty: 'I never was so near being beat'[268]. In 'a terrible fight for a terrible stake: freedom or slavery to Europe'[269] he had prevailed but only just. Every Allied soldier who fought in the Waterloo campaign contributed to that victory, and yet only the British and – often grudgingly – the Prussians have received proper recognition. But one-third of the men in Wellington's army were subjects of the King of the Netherlands, and even in their own countries few people have seemed aware of that fact.

The Dutch-Belgians faced a unique challenge long before June 1815 because of the circumstances of their recruitment. The Hanoverians, the Brunswickers and the King's German Legion formed cohesive units: they had already fought together, their drill was familiar, their officers trusted. The Duke had lost many of his crack Peninsular troops to the war in America and they were mostly replaced by inexperienced recruits – hence his remark about 'an infamous army' – but he still retained the nucleus of the force which the French had not been able to overwhelm. With the possible exception of De Lancey, he could rely completely not only on experienced, and often brilliant, subordinates such as Thomas Picton and Rowland Hill, but also on his more junior commanders – John Colborne, Colin Halkett and James Kempt – as well as his close aides, Fitzroy Somerset and Alexander Gordon; all of these had fought with him in the Peninsula. Finally he had comparatively few logistical problems – Baring's lack of ammunition at La Haie Sainte could be due to communication problems rather than those of actual supply – though he complained bitterly, as, in a familiar scenario, the politicians at home whittled down the supplies he demanded.

King Willem, on the other hand, had a mere eighteen months (January 1814 to June 1815 to recruit a national army, and less than a year (August 1814 to June 1815) to amalgamate two very different nationalities within that army. The archival material here (in both Dutch and French) shows his considerable achievement in fielding around twenty-five thousand troops, commanded by experienced and loyal officers for the Waterloo Campaign.

The lack of proper uniforms presented the Netherlanders with a further challenge. The Duke himself was indifferent to the fact that British uniforms varied widely even within the same regiment, but he expressed himself forcefully in 1811: 'I only beg that *we* may be as different as possible from the French in every thing.'[270] The Netherlanders were not so fortunate: the dark blue or dark green jackets, grey trousers and black shakos they wore made them indistinguishable from the French; through the swirling smoke and bewildering chaos of battle the British and (late on 18 June) the Prussians could hardly be expected to identify silver facings, yellow piping or the exact shape of headgear. Frequently only the desperate wave of an orange sash or glimpse of an orange cockade averted 'friendly fire', but there were plenty of instances where the perception came too late, most fatally when Picton's Highlanders opened up on Bijlandt's men at Quatre Bras.

That incident also highlights the further problems for an army of different nationalities – those of language and unfamiliarity with other units. Clear parade-ground orders bore little relevance to those issued in the heat of battle – refusal to obey orders, attributed to cowardice or treachery, might, just as easily, be due to misunderstanding or bewilderment. Baring tried in vain to pull back his mixed troops from the orchard to the safety of the farm buildings as the French drove forward, but 'my voice was unknown to them'; elsewhere on the field commands in any language could be 'lost in the thousands of repeated cries and drumming' while a deafening artillery barrage thundered from all sides.

The intelligence reports submitted to Wellington by the Prince of Orange and Rebècque show detailed and largely accurate reports of the French movements from the beginning of April, and it is clear from the records that their commanders acted accordingly. Barbero asserts flatly that Wellington's spies 'had given him no warning',[271] Grant's information certainly reached the Duke too late, but Wellington's discounting of the mass of information he did receive (for whatever reason) left him on the night of 15 June in one of the most dangerous situations of his military career – and it would be the distrusted Netherlanders who extricated him from it.

Had Saxe-Weimar not been alert enough to act on the intelligence he received and move down to Quatre Bras without orders on the late afternoon of 15 June, the French probe by the Red Lancers, which actually reached the crossroads within an hour of the Nassauers' arrival and was driven back by them, might have been followed through that same evening by the rest of the French left wing. The hypothesis that Ney's troops could have swept into an unsuspecting town still crowded with civilians is a valid one; even by the next morning the Duke's widely scattered army could hardly have stopped them.

Most historians now give 'the foreign troops' fair recognition for the initial stages of the battle of Quatre Bras, and move swiftly on to the undoubted courage and endurance of the British troops who reinforced them. Those reinforcements remembered it as a terrible battle in its own right, but the fact that, outnumbered by three to one, the Netherlanders had previously fought for two hours to give Wellington the time he needed, is too easily ignored.

There is no doubt that the Duke has often escaped criticism for his miscalculation before the Waterloo Campaign; the euphemism 'perhaps not at his best' has been employed. This study joins recent ones in defining his error more clearly. Without in any way underestimating his tactical genius during the battle of Waterloo, Wellington's strategic planning between mid-March and 15 June can be seen to be seriously flawed. Clausewitz's severe criticism, previously quoted, was written with hindsight but many junior commanders in the Allied Army worried at the time about the curious assumption of their superiors that Napoleon would simply wait in France to be attacked. British officers were restrained by respect or fear from questioning their commander's relaxed attitude, but the Netherlanders seem to have interpreted correctly every piece of intelligence they received.

The Duke's repeated insistence on 15–16 June that he must not risk making 'a false movement' resulted in a late reaction quite as dangerous as a premature concentration. One should use the word "obsession" very carefully, especially in the deadly context of hindsight, but the expectation of a flanking attack does seem to have dominated his thinking to the exclusion of everything else – the focus on Mons is a case in point since it would give the French that option, and it has even been suggested that Wellington's choice of Mont Saint Jean was to allow for a possible deployment to the right down the Nivelles road; as he rode down to Quatre Bras on the morning of 16 June in response to the alarming reports received overnight, he still did not urge the troops to move more quickly south. In addition, it should be remembered that at least ten thousand men of the Allied Army were never in action at all. Two divisions of II Corps spent 18 June at Hal, fifteen kilometres to the west under the command of Prince Frederik. Of the nine infantry divisions available to the Duke that day, they remained there as the rest of the army struggled to the narrowest of victories.

Some historians have given him the benefit of the doubt, pointing out the possibility of a French manoeuvre to the left, or emphasising the need to protect possible withdrawal to Ostend, although the nature of the terrain made it doubtful that those men at Hal could have marched north in time to protect much of what would have been a hasty retreat. With Napoleon apparently engaged on full-frontal attack, and surely unlikely to leave two large armies behind him, the likelihood of his launching a simultaneous flanking movement of any strength appears remote. As has been noted elsewhere, Wellington certainly expected the Prussians to arrive at Mont Saint Jean by mid-morning and communication with them was minimal as they fought their way towards him, but it does seem surprising that Prince Frederik's divisions were left unengaged, yet within reach.

The morning of 16 June saw the area west of Quatre Bras completely at a standstill as a heaving mass of five divisions of infantry, artillery and cavalry jostled and argued in the blazing heat along the single road through the village of Nivelles. There was further chaos even the next day as the units from furthest away headed up to Mont Saint Jean. The Netherlands cavalry action on the afternoon of 16 June was launched by exhausted men and animals immediately they reached the field, and was vilified by the British veterans whose own cavalry had had to travel furthest and therefore could only arrive when all was over late in the evening; the hussars had, until that morning, been cantoned sixty kilometres to the west. One can only echo the lament of Thomas Morris of the 73rd, 'should it have been so?'

Hamilton Williams asserts that '[Wellington's] staff had let him down badly over the concentration of his army',[272] but he had placed an impossible burden on them. After all, responsibility for the placement up to mid-June was the commander-in-chief's alone. Van der Capellan was a careful chronicler, and he certainly received the impression from the Duke that the whole army could be 'concentrated within six or eight hours'; the Prince of Orange assured Saxe-Weimar between five and six in the morning of 16 June 'that we would soon be supported by part of the English army',[273] (no reinforcements would arrive for nearly nine hours), while General Müffling informed Gneisenau at midnight on the 15/16 June that 'the Duke will be in the region of Nivelles in the morning with his whole force [sic] to support Your Highness'.[274]

The Duke of Wellington is, rightly, a towering figure in British history, but this should not make him immune from censure; initially the spread of his army over much of southern Belgium was valid, politically, logistically and strategically, but his misjudgement of Napoleon's intentions and his seeming distrust of the capacity of one-third of his army placed him very near to catastrophe on the night of 15 June. He owed a great debt to Rebècque, Perponcher and Saxe-Weimar, whose impressive alertness before, and military contribution during, Quatre Bras saved him from almost certain failure. He never admitted that contribution, and English-speaking historians have followed his lead, while those in the Netherlands have sought a voice in vain.

On the plateau of Mont Saint Jean on 18 June the Netherlanders no longer had to act alone and formed a vital element in the patchwork army which (just) won the victory. They fought across the whole length of the battlefield in the defence of Hougoumont, La Haie Sainte and Papelotte; and in two of the most perilous crises of the day their commanders, acting on their own initiative, came to the rescue of British regiments. Ghingy certainly saved Uxbridge's retreating cavalry from even worse disaster and inspired Vandeleur to follow him; and it was Chassé, not Peregrine Maitland nor John Colborne, who first launched a successful charge against the Imperial Guard – both these officers took it up, but it was his tremendous initial speed which saved the 30th and the 73rd as Macready acknowledges.

The performance of the Dutch, Belgian and Nassau officers exceeded all expectations, but most of them were experienced professionals; many of the men under their command were raw recruits, often inadequately equipped and trained, yet their "retreats" were hardly more numerous than British ones with a similar cause. Waterloo was remembered by Peninsular veterans as the most terrible battle of all, and one of the longest; certainly the artillery exchanges were the greatest ever experienced until that time; the Assistant Quartermaster General recorded the firing of seventeen thousand rounds of cannon shot.

A retired soldier, Cornelis de Jong van Rodenborgh, supervising the woodcutters on his farm near s'Hertogenbosch, a hundred and thirty five kilometres from Mont St. Jean, recalled,

> 'plotseling liggen ze met een oor op de grond. [Ik] volgt hun voorbeeld en nu hoort het donderend geweld van Napoleons laatste veldslag.'
>
> (*Suddenly they all lay with one ear to the ground.* [I] *followed their example and there heard the thunderous violence of Napoleon's last battle.*)[275]

Jon Jonxis renders in his own language an extract from Napoleon's dictated memoirs to Montholon, when recalling Quatre Bras:

> De Prins van Oranje heeft toen … het genie van de veldheer te bezitten; hem behoort de eer van de dag want zonder hem was het Engelsche leger vernietigd zonder slag geleverd te hebben en Blücher over den Rijn teruggeworpen zijn.
>
> (*The Prince of Orange proved on that day that he had the gifts of a warrior, the honour of the day belonged to him for without him the English army would have been wiped out without a fight, and Blücher could only have retreated across the Rhine.*)[276]

Napoleon's memory is not always to be trusted – after all most participants make the best case possible for their own actions – and as van Zanten points out, 'alles wat Bonaparte deed was politiek' (*everything Bonaparte did was political*): he continually demeans Wellington and Blücher, and, through them, Britain and Prussia as the victors, so that praise of the Netherlands diverted attention. On another occasion he referred to 'the heroic determination of the Prince of Orange [who] with a handful of men, dared to stand fast at Quatre Bras'; without that action 'I would have taken the English Army *in flagrante delicto*'.[277]

The French never concealed the participation of the Netherlanders. Their historian, Houssaye, lamented that at Waterloo the French had no chief of staff like Constant Rebècque and no general like Perponcher (the latter received the order of the Red Eagle from the King of Prussia). French and German sources have been far more honest in their Campaign accounts as far as the Netherlanders were concerned. In London, too, as the news of victory was received with relief and jubilation, there seemed at first to be praise for all. The Times leader of 21 June referred to

> the brave soldiers of the Low Countries [who] were not slow to prove otherwise than by words that they were resolved to conquer or to die for their sovereign and their country.[278]

However, attitudes rapidly changed as, in Jonxis' words, 'de Engelsche schreven de geschiedenis op hunne wijze' (*the English recorded history in their own way*).[279] National pride hardened into national bias, and prejudice was accepted as fact. Eventually it came to be

> seuls les Anglais furent heroiques, seuls ils ont vaincu le grand empereur, seuls ils ont envahi la France.
>
> (*only the English were heroic, only they defeated the great emperor, only they overran France.*)

Hofschröer's compelling attacks on the Duke could be a sign of the pendulum swinging too far, but it does provide a much-needed counterweight. "Mono-linguality" has led to grave injustice. The assertion 'that the troops of Wellington's army were, in the main, of nationalities other than British is forgotten, except, of course, where blame is imparted'[280] is a valid one.

Wellington's objection to all proposals to write a definitive history of

Waterloo was precisely that such individual stories might be used to reveal error (and perhaps also his own, as Hofschröer argues[281]) and thus affect reputations. The "myth" of Waterloo as a powerful symbol of Britain's place in Europe and the world, ensured that the British narrative was virtually unchallenged. English bias and distortion did sometimes rouse the Dutch to protest – an edition of Baedeker's Travel Guide to Holland in 1850 was challenged for its offensive assumptions. A Belgian serving officer protested in 1855 that a recent debate in the House of Commons had referred to 'auxiliaries who on that day [Waterloo] … did cowardly abandon their standards'; the term 'les braves Belges', he lamented, had become a byword for 'poltoonery'. He, at least, ensured an English translation, but in general lack of access to the Dutch language facilitated the steady shift from national history to national prejudice. (One of the very few Dutch books on Waterloo held by the British Library has many of its pages uncut.)

Dutch-Belgian officers at all levels had held high position in French service less than two years before the Waterloo campaign, and this background of changing allegiance is relevant to the reasons for such a lack of acknowledgement of the Netherlands contribution. These reasons may be understandable – linguistic, nationalistic or malicious – but they have contributed to a bias which is only now, after nearly two hundred years, beginning to be addressed. Many men of the Allied Army retreated or fled the fields of Quatre Bras and Waterloo: some were English or German, some were Dutch or Belgian, and the latter failures, so enthusiastically reported in the British memoirs which became the basis of British history, usually had the same terrible cause as the former ones – a fact too often suppressed.

Even after two hundred years there are still disputed facts about the Waterloo Campaign, and accounts of the same action differ widely. Too many attempts to simplify battlefield descriptions have resulted in what Keegan dismisses as 'choreography plus notations'.[282] The increasingly graphic descriptions of the Waterloo Campaign, which have marked the approach to the anniversary celebrations, make clear the full horror of that struggle for thousands of men whose world was limited to a few yards of swirling smoke, the roar of artillery and the appalling injuries to themselves or to the friends beside them; with very few exceptions every soldier who fought on those three days in June deserves respect and admiration. The British received both – to have survived Waterloo ensured immediate reverence; the French, thanks to Field, and the Prussians, through Hofschröer, have now received proper recognition outside their own countries, only the Netherlanders – to repeat, one-third of the Allied Army – have been denied a voice. Perhaps the reasons for that are now irrelevant if justice can at last be done – after all, it was the Duke of Wellington himself who said, 'there should be glory enough for all'.

Postscript

THIS STUDY HAS endeavoured to be fair to England's national hero while highlighting misjudgements already recognised by other historians, and suggesting a degree of deliberate concealment in his post-Campaign treatment of foreign allies. A more positive final note is probably due. One problem for the Great Duke, throughout his illustrious military career, was the necessity of working, not only with foreign allies, but with his own political masters – Napoleon, as head of state, had no such difficulty. The irresistible quotation below, from a book entitled *Warriors' Words*, is from a letter Wellington sent to the War Office from the Peninsula (with copies to every other government department) showing the pressure he was always under; it reveals a rather different man from the commander so often portrayed as severe and austere, respected by his men but never loved.

Gentlemen: While marching in Portugal to a position which commands the approach to Madrid and the French forces, my officers have been diligently complying with your request which has been sent by H.M. ship from London to Lisbon and then by despatch rider to our headquarters. We have enumerated our saddles, bridles, tents and tent poles, and all manner of sundry items for which His Majesty's Government holds me accountable. I have despatched reports on the character, wit, spleen of every officer. Each item and every farthing has been accounted for; with two regrettable exceptions for which I beg your indulgence. Unfortunately, the sum of one shilling and nine pence remains unaccounted for in one infantry battalion's petty cash, and there has been a hideous confusion as to numbers of jars of raspberry jam issued to one cavalry regiment during a sandstorm in western Spain. This reprehensible carelessness may be related to the pressure of circumstances since we are at war with France, a fact which may come as a bit of a surprise to you gentlemen in Whitehall. This brings me to my present purpose, which is to request elucidation of my instructions from His Majesty's Government so that I may better understand why I am dragging an army over these barren plains. I construe that perforce it must be one of the alternative duties, as given below. I shall pursue one with the best of my ability but I cannot do both. 1. To train an army of uniformed British clerks in Spain for the benefit of accountants and copy-boys in London, or, perchance, 2. To see to it that the forces of Napoleon are driven out of Spain.[283]

Notes

1 Geyl, p. 213.
2 Israel, p. 1120.
3 From van Wetering's memoirs which exist in a typescript copy in the Historischcentrum at Zwolle, p. 15.
4 Vels Heijn, p. 26. One promise 'weg met Douaniers' (away with the Customs Officers) was probably attractive.
5 Hofschröer, *1815 The German Victory,* vol. 1, p. 21.
6 Many Dutch exiles had accompanied the stadhouder's family to either London or Berlin.
7 Vels Heijn, p. 61.
8 Bew, p. 228.
9 Brownlow, p. 11.
10 Koninklijk Huisarchief (henceforth K.H.A.) A 35 xix 32.
11 In a letter to Earl Bathurst, Gurwood, vol. XII London (1838), p. 125.
12 Holmes, p. 214.
13 Wupperman, p. 216. An indication of the financial strain appears in Reuther's estimate of the cost of one wagon with four horses as 17,000 guilders, with two horses it was 11,000 but he warned that the latter were often not fit for purpose – a possible indication that both artillery and supply wagons at Waterloo were under-horsed to save money.
14 Extract from anniversary edition by de Grootmeester en de Inspecteur der Artillerie van de Koninklijk Landmacht (1939), p. 58.
15 McNab, p. 394.
16 Gurwood, p. 842.
17 Hamilton Williams, p. 140.
18 Clausewitz, *Hinterlassene werke über Krieg und Kriegfuhrung,* vol. XVII, p. 39. Translation by Hamilton Williams.
19 Oman, p. 632.
20 De Bas, pp. 251–2.
21 Pattison, p. 12.
22 Pawly, *Dutch Allies,* p. 20. This actually appears as 'an anonymous draft' of 2 April 1815 in *Supplementary Dispatches and Memoranda,* vol. X, p. 17.

23 Hofschröer, *The Smallest Victory*.
24 Field, p. 13.
25 Ibid, p. 14.
26 A Near Observer, *The Battle of Waterloo*, (Osprey Publishing, Oxford) 2013, p. 110.
27 Quoted in Field, op. cit., p. 19.
28 Houssaye, p. 22.
29 Creevey, p. 127.
30 Quoted by Longford, p. 355.
31 Quoted by Harvey, p. 743.
32 Gronow, p. 374.
33 Quoted by Brett James, p. 20.
34 Hamilton Williams, p. 89.
35 Hofschröer, *The German Victory*, p. 235.
36 Tomkinson, p. 146.
37 Clayton, p. 78.
38 Anglesey, p. 99.
39 K.H.A., A 34. h.
40 Holmes, p. 210.
41 W.D., vol. XII, pp. 312–13
42 In a letter to Lord Bathurst of 30 April 1815, quoted by Longford, p. 397.
43 W.D. vol. XII, p. 325.
44 Vels Heijn, p. 46.
45 Hansard April, 1815, quoted by Hamilton Williams, p. 76.
46 Barbero, p. 31.
47 *Gentlemans Magazine*, June, 1747.
48 Holmes, p. 169.
49 Blanco, p. 131.
50 K.H.A., A 40 xiii 10.
51 Nationaal Archief, 2.21.008.01., henceforth N.A.
52 It has to be said that the House of Orange showed some lack of imagination in their choice of first names – Willems and Frederiks appear regularly and confusingly in every generation which has occasionally caused confusion even in the Netherlands.
53 The Löben-Sels collection is a large one, totally unknown in English until 2010 when John Franklin used translators to publish a selection – *Netherlands Correspondence*.
54 Franklin, p. 60.
55 Wupperman, p. 9.
56 Bernard appears variously as Duke or Prince, a confusion perhaps due to the fact that the Congress of Vienna raised the rulers of many minor German states to the rank of Prince and he succeeded his father in 1828. Here, he will appear

simply as 'Saxe-Weimar' or 'Bernard' to distinguish him from Wellington and Orange and to avoid a foray into complicated German genealogies.

[57] Weller, p. 64, Robinson, p. 304.

[58] Bartels, p. 78.

[59] K.H.A., A 40 iv 60.

[60] K.H.A., A xix 26.

[61] Bartels, p. 84.

[62] Smith, vol. I, pp. 64–5. He saw active service from 1805–46.

[63] Douglas, p. 38.

[64] Letter from Charlotte, dated 16 June 1814, K.H.A., A 40 vi a 9.

[65] Bartels, p. 103.

[66] Quoted by Longford, p. 398.

[67] W.S.D., vol. X, pp. 167–8.

[68] Ensign Macready, quoted by Robinson, p. 50.

[69] Longford, op. cit., p. 398.

[70] De Bas and Wommersom, vol I, p. 175.

[71] W.S.D., vol. IX, pp. 593–610.

[72] von Müffling, introduction p. v.

[73] Louis Napoleon II, p. 338.

[74] K.H.A. Letter dated 28 March.

[75] It is an indication of the trust he and his father had in the returning 'French' officers that it was Van Merlen (ex-Imperial Guard) and Chassé whose patrols were stationed on the border – desertion, or, at the least, misinformation never seems to have been considered.

[76] Vels Heijn, p. 106.

[77] Report of Pieter van Zuijlen van Nyevelt, Franklin, p. 41.

[78] Robinson, p. 30.

[79] van Zuijlen, Franklin, p. 41.

[80] Hamilton Williams, p. 137.

[81] Holmes, p. 214.

[82] As regards Friedland, Napoleon had used his favourite phrase in a letter to his brother Joseph, describing his flanking manoeuvre and boasting that it had taken the enemy *in flagrante delicto*.

[83] In reply to questioning from Thomas Creevey, quoted in Longford, p. 404.

[84] Jennings, vol. 1, p. 343.

[85] Quoted by Hamilton Williams, p. 268.

[86] Holmes, p. 237.

[87] Longford, p. 405.

[88] Dallas, p. 122.

[89] N.A., 2. 21. 008. 01.

[90] Fouché, vol. 2, p. 341.

[91] N.A.2. 13.14.01.

92   Ibid.
93   Vels Heijn, p. 111.
94   Ibid. p. 106.
95   N.A. 2. 05. 01. nr. 771.
96   Gurwood, p. 854.
97   Robinson, p. 40.
98   Quoted by Holmes, p 222.
99   Franklin, p. 79.
100 De Bas quotes the full text, p. 240.
101 Mercer, p. 129.
102 Hofschröer, *The German Victory*, vol 1, p. 212.
103 Clayton, p. 145.
104 K.H.A., A 40 xiii 10.
105 Holmes, p. 227.
106 Longford, p. 419.
107 Vels Heijn, p. 117.
108 Jonxis, p 10.
109 Franklin, p. 80.
110 Robinson, p. 66.
111 Colonel Combes-Brassard, quoted by Field, p. 275.
112 Vels Heijn, p. 109. It should be noted that the jäger battalion had only joined him on 12 June.
113 Quoted by Robinson, p. 32.
114 Robinson, p. 89.
115 Hamilton Williams, p. 304.
116 Vels Heijn, p. 111.
117 K.H.A., A 40 xiii 10.
118 Robinson, p. 91.
119 N.A. 2.13.14. 01.
120 Jennings, p. 175.
121 Franklin, p. 77.
122 Major Richard Llewellyn of the 28th Regiment of Foot, writing in 1837.
123 Chandler, p. 11.
124 Hamilton Williams, p. 198.
125 Ibid., p. 197.
126 Robinson, p. 168.
127 Letter from Wijnand Koopman of the Dutch Horse Artillery to Löben-Sels, Franklin, p. 107.
128 De Bas, p. 515.
129 Robinson, p. 206.
130 Christemeijer, p. 21.
131 Robinson, p. 184.

132 Ibid., p. 315.

133 De Bas, p. 499.

134 Löben-Sels archive, Nr. II, no. 3.5.

135 Wakker's memoirs appear in a previously unregarded booklet in the Koninlijk Huisarchief, p. 3

136 Robinson, pp. 204–5.

137 Vels Heijn, p. 149.

138 Letter of 25 May 1841 to Löben-Sels, Franklin, p. 165.

139 De Bas, p. 462.

140 Pattison, p. 9.

141 Robertson, p. 148.

142 Chandler, p. 33.

143 Hofschröer, *German Victory*, vol. 1, p. 293.

144 Robinson, p. 291.

145 Robertson, p. 149.

146 Selby, pp. 68–69.

147 Robinson, p. 264.

148 Glover, p. 166.

149 Robinson, p. 310

150 Ibid., p. 338.

151 Ibid., p. 219.

152 Houssaye, p. 208.

153 Hamilton Williams, p. 219, note 39.

154 *W.S.D. vol.* x, p. 523.

155 Chesney, p. 129.

156 Weller, pp. 69–70.

157 *Vaderletteroefeningen,* p. 148.

158 Muir, p. 357.

159 Hamilton Williams, p. 221.

160 Robinson, p. 359.

161 Vallance, p. 9.

162 Wakker, pp. 8–10. The fact that the Prince himself attended to the provision of food to this unit seems to bear out the constant Netherlands complaint of lack of subsistence, and consequently focusses attention once more on the performance of the British general staff.

163 Franklin, pp. 144–45.

164 Quoted by Clayton, p. 337.

165 Mercer, p. 137–8.

166 Hibbert, p. 64.

167 Quoted by Field, p. 56

168 Wakker, p. 14.

169 van Wetering, p. 21.

[170] David, p. 465.

[171] British historians seem to have been as puzzled as Wellington was by the delayed arrival of the Prussians, and it is only recently that Hofschröer has fully examined the challenges they faced.

[172] Glover, *Archive,* p. 158.

[173] Longford, p. 451.

[174] Barbero, p. 322.

[175] Chandler, p. 53.

[176] David, p. 470.

[177] Hamilton Williams, p. 285.

[178] Magdalen and William de Lancey had been married less than two months when he was summoned to Brussels. On the outbreak of hostilities he sent her to Antwerp where she received the news that he was dead. This was untrue and she was able to nurse him in a cottage near the battlefield until he died a week later.

[179] Holmes, p. 211.

[180] De Lancey, p. 2.

[181] K.H.A., A 40. xiii 10.

[182] Chalfont, p. 95.

[183] Holmes, p. 241.

[184] Chandler, p. 57.

[185] Pawley, p. 39.

[186] Longford, p. 461.

[187] Shaw Kennedy, p. 111.

[188] Longford, ibid.

[189] Barbero, p. 166.

[190] Barbero, p. 171.

[191] Vels Heijn, p. 186.

[192] Franklin, p. 53.

[193] Cotton, p. 53.

[194] Longford, p. 461.

[195] Franklin, p. 64. A bayonet attack was used when the enemy was already in confusion after being raked by musketry. Contrary to many accounts, Bijlandt survived, and the quotation is from his letter of 31 May 1841.

[196] Wupperman, p. 127.

[197] *The Battle of Waterloo by a Near Observer,* p. 82.

[198] Quoted by Hamilton Williams, p. 304.

[199] Longford, p. 464.

[200] Barbero, p. 220.

[201] De Bas, vol. 3, p. 412. Quotation from a letter of 16 July 1823.

[202] Casper Morbotter, in a letter of 21 July 1841, Franklin, p. 161.

[203] Hope Pattison, p. 5.

[204] Franklin, p. 96.

[205] Franklin, ibid.

[206] Barbero, pp. 235–6.

[207] Hamilton Williams, p. 316.

[208] Quoted by Field, p. 168.

[209] Gronow, pp. 69–71.

[210] Keegan, p. 162.

[211] Vels Heijn, p. 175.

[212] Quoted by Barbero, p. 261.

[213] Franklin, p. 19.

[214] Weller, p. 121.

[215] Barbero, p. 324.

[216] Longford, p. 471.

[217] Barbero, p. 309. One criticism of his book has to be that for four hundred and twenty-four pages, he supplies just three and a half pages of notes and no references at all to justify such confident and nuanced assumptions as this one.

[218] Urban, p. 202.

[219] Hamilton Williams, p. 379, n. 39.

[220] A British officer, quoted by Clayton, p. 484.

[221] Quoted by Field, p. 187.

[222] There is confusion about the fate of Van Merlen – he was certainly severely wounded, but some accounts refer to him being carried off for medical treatment. He did not survive, but his body was never recovered.

[223] Howarth, pp. 164–5.

[224] Hofschröer, *The German Victory*, vol. II, p. 81.

[225] Barbero, p. 359.

[226] Quoted by Clayton, p. 507.

[227] Letter from Chassé, dated 27 April 1836, to Baron Charles Nepveu, former staff officer to Rebècque at Waterloo, Franklin, p. 115–16.

[228] Franklin, p. 138.

[229] Franklin, p. 132.

[230] Franklin, pp. 131–3.

[231] Davies, pp. 240–1.

[232] Letter, dated 4 July 1815, Franklin, p. 120.

[233] Houssaye, p. 398.

[234] Mercer, p. 180.

[235] Franklin, p. 148.

[236] N.A., 2. 21 .008 .01. 25.

[237] Franklin, p. 132.

[238] Hofschröer, *The German Victory*, vol. II, p. 127.

[239] Letter dated 29 August 1841 – Franklin, p. 97.

240 N.A., 2. 21. 008. 01. 25.

241 Longford, p. 488.

242 Müffling, p. 39.

243 Quoted by Field, p. 236

244 Hamilton Williams, p. 239.

245 Quoted by O'Keefe, p. 197.

246 *Gentleman's Magazine,* vol. 85, p. 73.

247 W.D., p. 549.

248 Muir, pp. 367–8.

249 W.S.D., VIII, p.175.

250 *Gentleman's Magazine,* vol. 85, p. 73.

251 Siborne, p. 341.

252 Hofschröer, p. 148.

253 Gurwood, p. 887.

254 Weller, p. 61.

255 Urban, *Rifles,* pp. 272–3

256 Roorda, M., pp. 26–7.

257 Wiegman, C., p. 67.

258 *Colburne's United Services Magazine,* September 1847, p. 6.

259 Clayton, p. 445.

260 Franklin, p. 120.

261 Franklin, p. 81.

262 Clayton, p. xvii.

263 Tomkinson, p. 286.

264 *Gentleman's Magazine,* vol. 85, p. 644.

265 Glover, *Waterloo Archive,* p. 63.

266 Franklin, p. 77.

267 P. J. Blok, *Geschiedenis van het Nederlandsche Volk,* p. 180.

268 Longford, p. 490.

269 Hope Pattison, p. 21.

270 W.D. VIII, pp. 371–2.

271 Barbero, p. 14.

272 Hamilton Williams, p. 221.

273 Franklin, p. 81.

274 Hamilton Williams, p. 178.

275 The quotation is from a review of the recent publication of van Rodenborgh's letters to his daughter, in the *NRC Handelsblad,* 28 December 2012.

276 Jonxis, p. 93.

277 From Napoleon's memoirs dictated to Count Montholon, quoted in *Army Quarterly and Defence Journal,* vol. 88 (1964).

278 *The Times,* 21 June 1815, quoted by Boulger, p. 8.

279 Jonxis, p. 105.

[280] Hofschröer, vol. I, p. 15.
[281] Hofschröer, *Smallest Victory.*
[282] Keegan, p. 187.
[283] Tsouras, pp. 51–2.

Bibliography

Manuscripts

Koninklijk Huisarchief, Den Haag, A35 xix 32, A 40 vi a 9, A 40 xiii 10.
Nationaal Archief, Den Haag, 2.02.01.6585, 2.05.01.771, 2.13.14.01.8, 2.21.008.01.
Löben-Sels, Stadsarchief, Zutphen, Nr. II.
Historischcentrum, Zwolle, memoir of Jan Willem van Wetering.

Primary Sources – Published

Anglesey, Marquess of, (ed.), *The Capel Letters, 1814–17,* (London) 1955.
Bain, Nicolson, *Detailed Account of the Battles of Waterloo and Quatre Bras,* (John Thomson and company, London) 1816.
Booth, L., *Battle of Waterloo,* (London) 1852.
Brett James, Anthony, (ed.), *Edward Costello, the Peninsular and Waterloo Campaigns,* (London) 1967.
Brett James, Anthony, ed., *The Hundred Days,* (London) 1964.
Brownlow, Emma, *The Eve of Victorianism,* (London) 1940.
Chesney, Charles, *Waterloo Letters,* (London) 1907.
Christemeijer (ed.), *Herinnering van een oud strijder,* (Utrecht) 1865.
Colenbrander, D., *Gedenkstukken der Algemeene Geschiedenis van Nederland, 1815–25,* (s'Gravenhage) 1915.
Cotton, Edward, *A Voice from Waterloo,* (London) 1841.
De Lancey, Magdalene, *A Week at Waterloo,* (London) 2008.
Douglas, John, *Tales of the Peninsula and Waterloo,* (London) 1997.
Field, Andrew, *Waterloo: the French Perspective,* (Pen and Sword) 2012.
Fouché, Joseph, *Mémoires de Joseph Fouché,* (Paris) 1944.
Franklin, John, (ed.) *Waterloo, Netherlands Correspondence,* vol. 1 (1815 Limited) 2010.
Gronow, Rees Howell, *Reminiscences and Recollections,* (London) 1892.
Gurwood, John, *Dispatches of Field Marshal the Duke of Wellington,* (London) 1834–38.

Hibbert, Christopher (ed.), *The Diary of Edmund Wheatley*, (London) 1964.

Jennings, Louis, (ed.) *Correspondence and Diaries of John Wilson Croker*, (London) 1888.

Kincaid, John, *Adventures in the Rifle Brigade*, (London) 1830.

Liddell Hart, Basil, (ed.) *The Letters of Private Wheeler*, (London) 1951.

Maxwell, Herbert, (ed.), *The Creevey Papers*, (London) 1904.

McGrigor, James, *Autobiography*, (London) 1861.

Mercer, Alexander Cavalié, *Journal of the Waterloo Campaign*, (Edinburgh) 1870.

Moore Smith, G. (ed.) *Autobiography of General Sir Harry Smith,* (London) 1910.

Napoleon, Louis, (ed.), *Memoires de la Reine Hortense*, 2 vols., (Paris) 1827.

Pattison, Frederick Hope, *Personal Recollections of the Waterloo Campaign*, (Glasgow) 1873.

Rem, Jan, *Aantekeningen van een veteaan*, (Purmerend) 1865.

Robertson, David, *Journal of Sergeant Robertson, late 92nd Foot*, (Perth) 1842.

Schom, Alan, *One Hundred Days*, (Michael Joseph, London) 1993.

Selby, John, (ed.), *Memoirs of Thomas Morris*, (Moreton-in-Marsh) 1998.

Shaw Kennedy, James, *Notes of the Battle of Waterloo*, (London) 1865.

Siborne, William, *The Waterloo Letters*, reprint, (London) 1983.

Tomkinson, William, *Diary of a Cavalry Officer in the Peninsular and Waterloo Campaigns,* (London) 1894.

Vaderlandsche Letteroefeningen, (Amsterdam) *1816* – a collection of contemporary letters.

Vane, Charles, (ed.) *Correspondence and Dispatches of Viscount Castlereagh,* vol. X, (London) 1850.

Von Müffling, *A Sketch of the Battle of Waterloo*, (London) 1870.

Wakker, Pieter, *Aantekeningen van een veteran*, (J Schuitermaker, Purmerend) 1863.

Wellington, 2nd Duke of, (ed.), *Supplementary Dispatches,* (London) 1858–72.

Wiegmans, C., *Aantekeningen van Quatre Bras en Waterloo*, (D. Allart, Amsterdam) 1865.

Newspapers and Journals

Army Quarterly and Defence Journal, vol. 88 (1964) – extract from Montholon's memoirs of Napoleon.

Brussels Herald, (July 1855), defence of Belgium by 'a serving officer'.

Gentleman's Magazine, (June, 1747), account of the battle of Val.

NRC Handelsblad, (28 December, 2012), review of van Rodenborgh letters.

Nineteenth Century Magazine, (October 1900), Charles Oman rebuke to Herbert Maxwell.

Ons Leger, (Den Haag) 1939.

Vorsten Historie, (February, 1990).

The Times, (21 June, 1815).

The 19th News (1892) Dixon Vallance.

Secondary Sources

Anon. *A Hanoverian Officer one hundred years ago*, (London) 1898.

Adkin, Mark, *The Waterloo Companion*, (Aurum, London) 2001.

Barbero, Alessandro, *The Battle*, (London) 2005.

Bartels, Jacques, 'De Erfprins in Britse Krijgsdienst', *Oranje Jaarboek*, (Den Haag) 2004.

Bew, John, *Castlereagh, Enlightenment, War and Tyranny*, (London) 2011.

Blanco, Richard, *Wellington's Surgeon General, Sir James McGrigor*, (Durham, N.C.) 1974.

Blok, P. J., *Geschiedenis van der Nederlandse Volk*, (Sijthoff, Leiden) 1925.

Boulger, Demetrius, *The Belgians at Waterloo*, (London) 1901.

Chalfont, Alan, ed., *Waterloo, Battle of Three Armies*, (New York) 1980.

Chandler, David, *Waterloo, the Hundred Days*, (London) 1993.

Clayton, Tim, *Waterloo*, (London) 2014.

Corrigan, Gordon, *Wellington*, (London) 2001.

Dallas, Gregor, *1815, the Roads to Waterloo*, (London) 1996.

David, Saul, *All the King's Men*, (London) 2012.

Davies, Huw, *Wellington's Wars*, (Yale, London) 2012.

Davies, Norman, *A History of Europe*, (Oxford) 1996.

De Bas, F. and De T'Serclaes Wommersom, J., *La campagne de 1815 aux Pays-Bas*, 3 vols., (Brussels) 1908.

Foulkes, Nick, *Dancing into Battle*, (London) 2007.

Geyl, Pieter, *Willem IV en Engeland tot 1748*, (Den Haag) 1924.

Glover, Gareth, (ed.), *Unpublished Letters from the Siborne Papers*, (London) 2004.

Glover, Gareth, *Waterloo Archive*, 5 vols., (Barnsley) 2010–13.

Griffith, Paddy, *French Napoleonic Infantry Tactics*, (London) 2007.

Hamilton Williams, David, *Waterloo, New Perspectives*, (London) 1999.

Harvey, Robert, *War of Wars*, (London) 2006.

Haythornwaite, Philip, *Uniforms of Waterloo*, (London) 1974.

Haythornwaite, Philip, *The Armies of Wellington*, (London) 1998.

Hofschröer, Peter, *1815: The German Victory*, 2 vols., (Pennsylvania) 2001.

Hofschröer, Peter, *Wellington's Smallest Victory*, (London) 2004.

Holmes, Richard, *Wellington, the Iron Duke*, (London) 2002.

Howarth, David, *Waterloo*, (London) 1968.

Houssaye, Henri, *Waterloo*, (Perrin et co., Paris) 1898.

Israel, Jonathan, *The Dutch Republic, 1477–1806*, (Clarendon Press, Oxford) 1995.

Jonxis, J. P., *Quatre Bras*, (Doesborgh) 1875.

Keegan, John, *The Face of Battle*, (London) 1976.

Knoop, Willem Jan, *Beschouwingen over Siborne's Geschiedenis van den oorlog van 1815 in Frankrijk en Nederland en wederlegging van de in dat werk voorkomende beschuldigingen tegen het Nederlandse leger*, (Breda) 1846.

Koch, Jeroen, *Koning Willem I*, (Boom, Amsterdam) 2013.

Logie, Jacques, *Waterloo, the Campaign of 1815*, (Spellmount, Stroud) 2003.

Longford, Elizabeth, *Wellington: the Years of the Sword*, (London) 1968.

Maxwell, Herbert, *The Life of Wellington*, 2 vols., (London) 1898.

McNab, Chris, (ed.), *Armies of the Napoleonic Wars*, (London) 2009.

Muir, Rory, *The Path to Victory*, (Yale, New York) 2013.

O'Keefe, Paul, *Waterloo, The Aftermath*, (London) 2014

Pawly, Ronald, *Wellington's Belgian Allies*, (London) 2001.

Pawly, Ronald, *Wellington's Dutch Allies*, (London) 2002.

Robinson, Mike, *The Battle of Quatre Bras*, (Spellmount, Stroud) 2009.

Roorda, Marten, *Historie Vorsten*, 1990.

Summerville, Christopher, *Who Was Who at Waterloo*, (Pearson Education Ltd) 2007.

Tsouras, P. G., *Warriors' Words*, (London) 1992.

Urban, Mark, *Rifles*, (London) 2003.

Van Zanten, Jeroen, *Koning Willem II*, (Boom, Amsterdam) 2013.

Vels Heijn, Nicolaas, *Glorie zonder Helden*, (Amsterdam) 1974.

Von Pivka, Oscar, *Dutch-Belgian Troops of the Napoleonic Wars*, (Oxford) 2000.

Webster, Anthony, *Debate on the Rise of the British Empire*, (Manchester) 2006.

Weller, Jac, *Wellington at Waterloo*, first published 1967, new edition (London) 1998.

Wooten, Geoffrey, *Waterloo, 1815*, (London) 1992.

Wupperman, Willem, *De Vorming van der Nederlandsche Leger na de opwenteling van 1813 en het aandeel van dat leger aan de Veldtocht van 1815*, (Breda) 1900.

Index

Plate 1: King Willem I of the Netherlands (Royal Archive, The Hague ref. no. SK-A-4113)
Frederick Bury, 1808.

He adopts the romantic mode, and also, perhaps, imitates Napoleon by placing his hand inside
the cloak. He wears the Prussian Black Eagle, despite an ignominious end to his military career.
His mother found the hairstyle absurd, writing to him, 'It distresses me that no one recognises
you … how true is the proverb, "the balder you are, the handsomer you are"'. When she later
issued the painting as a print after his accession, the tufted hair was flattened.

The Figures by T.Rowlandson. — Architecture by I.Shephard.

Engraved by R.Reeves.

Plate 2: The Patriotic Dinner (Royal Archive, The Hague PR/2171) Thomas Rowlandson, Rudolph Ackerman, 1st January 1814. 'Representation of the Meeting held at the City of London Tavern, on 14th December, 1813, to celebrate the glorious Event of the Emancipation of Holland from the Usurpation of the 'Tyrant of France'. Presiding were the Duke of Clarence and the Prince of Orange 'having returned only the day before from Lord Wellington's army'. The 'Tavern' in Bishopsgate was built in 1768 to be used by the livery companies – three hundred tickets were issued for this occasion, and the guests are shown drinking the health of their 'old Friends and Allies, the Dutch … with enthusiastic joy'.

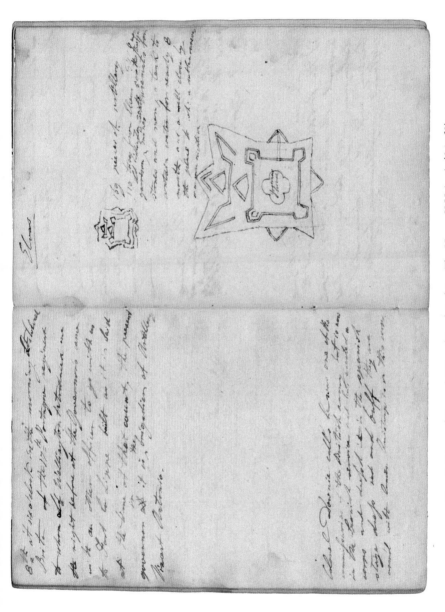

Plate 3: Prince of Orange's Diary (Royal Archive, The Hague K.H.A., A 40.iv.60).

Plate 4: The Battle of Quatre Bras
(Royal Archive, The Hague SC/0715)
Jan Willem Pieneman, 1818.

Before the British reinforcements arrive the Prince of Orange signals for his first charge. The chestnut horse (which would be killed at Waterloo) has already trampled one of the enemy and on the right a Dutch militiaman pins the cuirassier to the ground. The Prince's staff are grouped behind him and the officer on the grey is probably Perponcher. On the left an infantryman from a line regiment whose shako plate proclaims 'Voor Koning en Vaderland', advances to attack.

Pieneman always concentrates on facial expressions: in the 1820s he travelled to London to paint small portraits of all Waterloo officers. These he combined in an enormous group portrait which he tried to sell to Wellington in 1824 – the Duke refused and it now hangs in the Rijksmuseum.

Plate 5: The Battle of Quatre Bras (Royal Archive, The Hague PR2173)

British reinforcements are at last on the field – the first to arrive were Picton's Highlanders who were badly mauled. The Prince of Orange, beside the banner, glances back at men trying to cut the traces of a possible supply wagon as the horses have gone down. In the middle distance is the steeply sloping roof of the barn of Piraumont farmhouse to the south-east of Quatre Bras which French troops are skirting to the left, and the 95th Regiment of Foot are preparing a flanking attack on them.

Plate 6: The Battle of Quatre Bras (Royal Archive, The Hague PR2174) Jan Anthonie Langendijk.

This shows the moment of the Prince of Orange's second charge at Quatre Bras. The green uniformed troops on the left are the 27th Jäger and the 5th Militia; while casualties from their first charge are clearly visible, the Prince, about to mount his horse, summons them to follow him which they did 'to a man'. At the bottom right is the wreckage of one of the very few artillery pieces on the field, while some of the late arriving British reinforcements can be seen in the middle distance.

Plate 7: The Duke of Wellington at Waterloo (Royal Archive, The Hague PR/2194) Jean Baptiste Madou.

Plate 8: The Battle of Waterloo (Royal Archive, The Hague PR2175) Joseph Denis Odevaere, 1817

The Prince of Orange is struck by a musket ball in the shoulder while leading a charge as the fate of the battle hung in the balance. His staff rush to rescue him, but the most interesting feature is the captured French eagle on the left carried by Corporal Styles of the 1st Royal Dragoons. This incident happened much earlier but is placed alongside the Prince's wounding because the picture was presented 'with the most profound respect' to his mother, Queen Frederica Louise, originally a Princess of Prussia. The battle-honour of Jena as the most traumatic of Napoleon's victories over the Prussians is thus significant.